"Aliza Sherman is a force and inspiration! Her valuable *PowerTools* go beyond tech and teach what it really takes to make positive change happen."

> —Robin Fisher Roffer, author of *Make a Name for Yourself* and president, Big Fish Marketing, Inc.

"No matter what topic Aliza Sherman writes about, she always finds a way to empower and inspire women to not only make a difference in their own lives, but also in the lives of others. With *PowerTools for Women in Business*, she's once again proven herself a force to be reckoned with."

> —Hillary Carlip, author of *Girl Power: Young Women Speak Out* and Co-President/Founder of Voxxy, Inc.

"*PowerTools* is an inspirational book that encourages a woman to go 'against the odds,' and create her own 'success formula:' running a business she loves but still having time for a life filled with family, friends, and her community."

> —Priscilla Y. Huff, "*Self-Employed Woman*," columnist and author of *101 Best Home-Based Businesses for Women* and HerVenture.com.

"Chock full of powerful advice, this book will inspire and motivate you to take charge of your future and create a life you love. If you want to drive your own destiny, read this book."

> —Elizabeth Carlassare, author of *Dotcom Divas: E-Business Insights from the Visionary Women Founders of 20 Net Ventures*

"Success-minded people will benefit greatly from Aliza Sherman's insights and strategies."

> — Jane Applegate, author of *201 Great Ideas for Your Small Business* and founder SBTV.com

"Aliza Sherman's new book covers many of the issues that women, not just businesswomen, face on their life paths. The stories in her book are moving and inspirational."

—Lynne Franks, author of *The SEED Handbook*,
Founder/President of Globalfusion

"*PowerTools* presents a rich battery of down-to-earth and common-sensical techniques that women can use to create more satisfying ways of working and living. Bravo Aliza!"

—Sally Helgesen of author, *The Female Advantage*
and *Thriving in 24/7*

"Aliza has been there from the beginning. A tour-de-force of the Internet—empowering women to greet new technology with open arms. Now she's doing the same thing for women in business. Buy this book!"

—Meredith Bagby, author of *Rational Exuberance:
The Influence of Generation X on the New American
Economy* and *We've Got Issues: The Get-Real, No
B.S., Guide to What Really Matters*

"*PowerTools for Women in Business* is a must-read book for everyone. Aliza Sherman's utterly clever advice and strategies can help anyone realize their dreams. Read it, use it and empower your life."

—Danny Seo, author of *Heaven on Earth* and
Be the Difference

"Aliza Sherman's *PowerTools for Women in Business* is an empowering tour de force that celebrates women's unique ability to leverage business savvy with passion and intuition in order to succeed in business and in life. *PowerTools* encourages women to trust their instincts and inner voice as well as their smarts."

—Jodi Turek, President and cofounder,
womens-forum.com

"An insightful, informative, and ultimately inspiring book about how women not only can succeed in business, but also draw on their true passions to do so. Through sharing her experiences and those of other successful businesswomen—and by outlining detailed "Personal Projects" to help readers jumpstart their careers—Aliza Sherman offers a truly groundbreaking book for any woman who has ever wondered how to navigate through the business world."

> —Lucy McCauley, editor of *Travelers' Tales: Women in the Wild* and contributing editor at *Fast Company* magazine

"*PowerTools* is an absolute must-read for businesswomen. Aliza Sherman shows you how to expand your career vision, and she gives you a practical process to make your dreams come true."

> —Kate Ludeman, Ph.D., co-author, *The Corporate Mystic*

"Very valuable and inspirational stories that not only detail the advice of successful entrepreneurial role models, but also provide meaningful action plans and resources to keep the woman business-owner motivated."

> —Marsha Firestone, Ph.D., President, Women Presidents' Organization

Aliza is the one person who understood how women needed technology from the start—back when the naysayers thought it was all so unnecessary. Now that the world has caught up, Aliza's deeper insights are coming into play. Her new work is the evolution of positive and usable strategies, now available in book form!

> —Richard Laermer, CEO, RLM Public Relations, author of book series *Native's Guide To New York*

"Aliza Sherman's *PowerTools for Women in Business* will clearly benefit women with many different interests and ambitions. I like the fact that the *PowerTools* includes advice about women's power and the importance of integrating our hearts into everything we do."

— Connie K. Duckworth, Advisory Director,
Goldman Sachs and Company

"Aliza Sherman is a powerhouse of information and inspiration, and she is once again on the pulse of the challenges facing women today. Her hands-on experiences and those of others offer insightful understanding of the commonalities amongst women, and how it is possible to create a fulfilling life by adopting a strategic approach that includes the sharing of knowledge, resources, and support. Armed with *PowerTools*, any goal becomes possible."

— Robin Gorman Newman, founder of www.Love Coach.com, and author of *How to Meet a Mensch in New York*

Diane~

Here's to wielding our power well & never losing what makes us so unique.

STRENGTH!

PowerTools SM
for **WOMEN** *in*
BUSINESS

Aliz Sherman

12-12-01
Cheyenne

PowerTools^{SM}
for WOMEN in BUSINESS

10 Ways to Succeed in Life and Work

ALIZA SHERMAN

EP

Entrepreneur. Press

Editorial Director: Jere Calmes
Cover and Interior Design: Beth Hansen-Winter
Production: Eliot House Productions
Composition: Beth Hansen-Winter
Cover photograph by John Emerson (NYC)

This publication is designed to provide accurate and authoritative information
in regard to the subject matter covered. It is sold with the understanding that the
publisher is not engaged in rendering legal, accounting, or other professional
services. If legal advice or other expert assistance is required, the services of a
competent professional person should be sought.

Library of Congress Cataloging-in-Publication Data
Sherman, Aliza.
PowerTools for women in business: 10 ways to succeed in life and work/Aliza
Sherman.
         p.   cm.
Includes bibliographical references and index.
ISBN 1-891984-32-2
1. Businesswomen—Life skills guides. 2. Computers and women. 3. Internet.
4. Success in business. I. Title: PowerTools for women in business. II. Title.

HD6053.S53 2001
650.1'082—dc21   2001023242   CIP

Printed in Canada
09 08 07 06 05 04 03 02 01   10 9 8 7 6 5 4 3 2 1

Dedication

"Women indeed know their place.
It's at the helm of their very own companies."
—Janean Chun

TO MY DAD, MOM, SISTER, FERNE, AND ESE,
THE BEST SUPPORT NETWORK A GIRL COULD EVER WANT.

In memory of my Mexican Grandmother
Pasquala Vasquez Enriquez
1901–1995
An Entrepreneurial Woman

CONTENTS

Foreword by Sandra Hernandez Adams   xvii

Preface by Orit   xix

Acknowledgments   xxi

INTRODUCTION   1

What Are the PowerTools?

Understanding the PowerTools

Birth of the PowerTools

Sharing PowerTools

How to Use this Book

CHAPTER 1: *Share Your Stories—Teach, Inspire, Motivate, and*
Learn by Telling and Listening   7

Storytelling as My Catalyst

Why Tell Your Stories?

SHE READS: *Kate Moon, Walkabout Comfort Shoe Store*

Honoring Our Stories

Personal Project #1: *Life Story Titles*

Personal Project #2: *The Gathering*

A Real-Life Gathering of Women

A Few Days Later

A Few Months Later

NUGGETS: *Books of Women's Stories*

Books on Writing Your Life Story

Websites about Herstory

PowerTool 1 Checklist

CHAPTER 2: *Take Charge of Change—Make Change Happen Rather Than Letting It Run Your Life and Business* 23

Change in My Own Life

Change Happening to You

Discovering What to Change

Making Change Happen

Personal Project #1: *Deploy the Mini-Change Agent*

Personal Project #2: *The Placement of Things*

    NUGGETS: *Books on Feng Shui*

                Web Sites on Feng Shui

PowerTool 2 Checklist

CHAPTER 3: *Never Stop Learning—It's Never Too Late to Discover Something New* 39

Learning My Way

The Value of Traditional Learning

Nontraditional Learning

    E-QUOTE: *Sherry Harsch-Porter, Porter Bay Group*

Learning by Doing

Learning about Yourself

Solo Adventuring

Personal Project #1: *Honor the Student Within*

Personal Project #2: *The Solo Adventure for the Soul*

    NUGGETS: *My Favorite Books on Women's Solo Travels*

                Business Books I Recommend

                General Courses Online

                Business Courses Online

PowerTool 3 Check List

CHAPTER 4: *Overcome Crisis—And Use It to Gain Wisdom*   59

My Own Crisis

Turning Around Professional Crisis

Rising Up from Personal Crisis

If You Don't Have Your Health

The Unexpected Accident

Hitting Too Close to Home

Coping with the Emotional Split

Like a Phoenix

Personal Project #1: *The Essential "You" Day*

Personal Project #2: *Journaling for Healing*

NUGGETS: *Books asbout Creative Writing and Journaling*
Female Motivational Speakers

PowerTool 4 Checklist

CHAPTER 5: *Tackle Technology—Make It Your Tool to Help*
Accomplish Your Goals   79

Touching Technology

Turning the Internet into My Tool

From "No Skills" to Tech Biz

E-QUOTE: *Michelle Lawlor, eKindness.com*

Starting a "Dotcom"

The Internet as "Essential Business Tool"

E-QUOTE: *Lorraine M. Pasquali, ImagineStation*

Personal Project #1: *Build a Web Site of Your Own*

Personal Project #2: *Teach Someone How to Go Online*

NUGGETS: *Books to Teach Yourself Basic Web Building*

Web Sites with HTML Tutorials

Free Web Sites

PowerTool 5 Checklist

CHAPTER 6: ***Mold Your Mission—Write Down Your Life's Purpose and Make It Real***   95

My Lifelong Dream

From Dream to Mission

Living and Working by a Mission

The Care and Feeding of Your Mission

    SHE READS: *Joy Radle, All MarCom, LLC*

A Motto for Your Mission

Business Missions Get Personal

Formulating Your Mission

Personal Project #1: *Make Your Motto*

Personal Project #2: *Business Plan for Your Life*

    NUGGETS: *Books on Business Plans*

               Web Sites on Business Plans

PowerTool 6 Checklist

CHAPTER 7: ***Be a Mentor—Take Time to Teach and Be a Role Model***   117

In Search of Role Models

My Accidental Mentors

Searching for a Female Mentor

E-Mentoring as an Option

The Art of Mentoring

Influencing Others

The Value of Mentors

Personal Project #1: *Find a Mentor*

Personal Project #2: *Be a Mentor*

NUGGETS: *Books on Mentoring*

Web Sites on Mentoring

PowerTool 7 Checklist

Chapter 8: **Nurture Your Network—Cultivate It and It Will
Nourish You**   131

Discovering Networking

Networking, My Way

Networking According to Lucy Rosen

The Need/Give Philosophy

Networking in Action

E-QUOTE: *Kathleen Zemaitis, Zine Communications*

Creating Network Circles

Personal Project #1: *Name Tag Tricks*

Personal Project #2: *Play Matchmaker, Matchmaker*

NUGGETS: *Books about Networking*

Web Sites about Networking

PowerTool 8 Checklist

CHAPTER 9: **Wield Your Power—Revel in Your
Accomplishments and Brag**   145

The Truth about Power

Oh, It's Nothing Really

I'm Sorry, You Go Ahead

The Male/Female Dynamic

Women and Power

    SHE READS: *Alexandria K. Brown, AKB & Associates*

Brag, Brag, Brag

    E-QUOTE: *Kimberly L. McCall, McCall Media and Marketing, Inc.*

Personal Project #1: *Write Your CV*

Personal Project #2: *Make Your Own Media Kit*

Personal Project #3: *Speak in Public*

    NUGGETS: *Books on Public Speaking*

                 Web Sites for Public Speaking

PowerTool 9 Checklist

CHAPTER 10: ***Give Back—When You've Got It,
Spread It Around***   163

    SHE READS: *Trish Patterson, DCSSA*

The Art of Giving

    E-QUOTE: *Heather O'Neil, eTravelplan.com*

Your Community, Your World

Personal Project #1: *Choose a Cause*

Personal Project #2: *Spring Clean for Charity*

    E-QUOTE: *Nancy Lublin, Dress for Success*

    NUGGETS: *Web Sites for Online Giving*

PowerTool 10 Check List

CHAPTER 11: ***It Starts With You—Honor Your True Self
and the Rest Will Follow***   175

My PowerTools List

APPENDIX: ***The Women in this Book***   179

FOREWORD

WHEN I FIRST READ THE UNPUBLISHED MANUSCRIPT FOR *Power-Tools*, I was instantly reminded of my own "Rules of Life." About 20 years ago I began documenting my own "Rules of Life" as a guide and reminder of those things that influence how I think, feel, behave, and respond.

Some of my Rules are based on observations. For example, one of my Rules simply states that "Your strength is also your weakness." That Rule reminds me that often times an admired personal trait in someone is generally the same trait or characteristic that is their Achilles heel.

The second thing that struck me about Aliza's *PowerTools* is that these are tools for everyday life. While it is true that the general context of the book is business focused, these tools should be applied to our daily lives. She mentions that fact throughout the book, but I often wonder if people realize how raising children can be so similar to managing employees. This, of course, does not imply that we should treat our employees as children; but it does remind us that like our children, employees need guidance, goals, security, consistency, boundaries, direction, and motivation.

Lastly, I am struck by Aliza's inclusion of stories and experiences from other women. I feel that the Power in the *PowerTools* title really comes from the shared value systems, dreams, experiences, and life stories. No matter how often we tell ourselves that we are not alone in our struggles, it is somehow encouraging when we are reminded that our fears and foibles have already been experienced by someone else and no matter how dark the moment, we can be encouraged when the moment is shared.

Aliza's *PowerTools* will inspire readers to reach and stretch just a little higher. Her *PowerTools* serve to remind us of things we already know but are helpful in their simplicity giving us the ability to put them into Action in our own lives.

This book will inspire you, encourage you, teach you, and guide you.

—Sandra Hernandez Adams, President, Strategic Micro
Partners and President, National Association for
Women Business Owners (NAWBO)

PREFACE

As president of the National Association of Women Business Owners (NAWBO), New York City chapter, I'm involved with women and their stories on a day to day basis. It's amazing the volume of e-mails and calls I receive every day from women seeking advice, support, and affirmation for their individual and collective endeavors.

Women are not afraid to ask each other for help—this is what makes us so strong.

The way that Aliza has structured *Power Tools* allows the reader to benefit from its wisdom in a very interactive way—the anecdotes are inspirational because they are real stories that we can relate to—in the same way we relate to our mentors.

The skill sets are crucial to succeeding as an entrepreneur, both professionally and personally—networking, setting goals, embracing change as opportunity. These lessons are invaluable, but they don't have to be learned the hard way—here is a resource that demonstrates, as Aliza so eloquently describes, "storytelling as a catalyst."

The stories collected in *Power Tools* were encouraging for me because it's easy to become so focused on the day-to-day that you don't think about all that you've accomplished. Reading about how other women beat the odds and worked to succeed at realizing their dreams not only impressed me, but also helped me to put my own achievements in perspective. Relating your own story to someone else's is validating. It also helps you to take stock in yourself and recognize your potential.

An integral part of recognizing your potential has to be discovering your passion. Ultimately, you will measure your success by how much of yourself you have invested, and we invest in what we love. Not everyone has what it takes to be an entrepreneur—we all have unique abilities. Everyone, however, has the capacity to follow her passion. The stories chronicled here are proof and inspiration. You have to WANT it—this is what will drive you to succeed in whatever you do. The *PowerTools* are a means of guiding you towards finding that energy and making it work for you.

> —Orit, President of the National Association of Women Business Owners (NAWBO), New York City chapter President and CEO, The O Group

ACKNOWLEDGMENTS

THANK YOU TO ALL AT ENTREPRENEUR MEDIA AND ENTREPRENEUR Press, especially Rieva Lesonsky, Marla Markman, Kim White and Jere Calmes, for believing in the PowerTools.

Special thanks to my book agent Lisa Swayne, Susan Barry, and all at the Swayne Agency for always going beyond the call of duty.

Super thanks to esteemed colleagues, good friends, and kick-ass women who have inspired or helped me in some way down the path of my life, including Alison Berke, Laura Brandt, Hillary Carlip, Toni Cline, Jeanne Cluess, Paulette Cooper, Sara Cross, Susan Defife, Wendy Dubit, Connie Duckworth, Renee Edelman, Monique Elwell, Donna Ferrato, Susan Gessner, Lisa Gill, Sherrye Henry, Brenda Kahn, Maria Kalligeros, Angela Kapp, Jenai Lane, Amy Langer, Lori Levine, Ellen LaNicca, Cindy Lupatkin, Anna Mangum, Rachel Masters, Yvonne Mojica, Amy Ormond, Ellen Pearlman, Courtney Pulitzer, Annie (AMP) Pennola, Eva Shaderofsky, Shelley Shaw, Lisa Skriloff, Tery Spataro, Pat Sterling, Patrice Tanaka, Michelle Van Gilder, Marsha Vlasic, Linda Walker, Sara Weinheimer, and Sharon Zadanoff. Thanks also to superguys Samir Arora, Cliff Burnstein, Jerry Colonna, Michael Diamant, Charlie Jackson, Kevin Kennedy, Richard Laermer, Robert Levitan, Peter Mensch, Alberto Perez, and Danny Seo, just to name a few.

And to all of the women profiled within these pages: Your generosity and willingness to share will hopefully inspire millions, either through this book or through your actions and encounters every day. This book is for you.

INTRODUCTION

NO MATTER WHAT OUR BACKGROUNDS, STATUS, CULTURE, OR PERsonal or professional experiences, we often face self-imposed and external obstacles that stand in the way of our true path or success. How can we move forward, learn, grow, and succeed in business in a way that is in line with our deepest values and goals?

First we must get in touch with what we really want in our lives. Then we must take positive steps each day that direct us to what we want out of both our businesses and our lives. But where do we begin?

I have looked at my own life and business while writing this book and seen definite moments when I took actions that got me closer to my true purpose. But there were also too many other moments when I took a wrong turn or made a random choice, or when forces "beyond my control" got in the way.

So how did I become a full-time writer and speaker, my lifelong dream? I made some deliberate and conscious choices in my life, and began to live by some common-sense rules that I call my "PowerTools."

WHAT ARE THE POWERTOOLS?

A PowerTool is part advice and part strategy. It is not only a rule to live by, but a clear step you can take to improve the way you work and live. By applying the PowerTools, you can move your life and business forward in more exciting and fulfilling ways. Most importantly, you can create the business you want that fits your life instead of having to constantly compromise.

Many of the PowerTools may sound familiar to you. They might be variations of advice you've heard from your parents or a teacher, friend, or mentor. You may have even skimmed the list of the PowerTools and thought, "I already know that" or "that's so obvious." But can you honestly say that you live by them, consciously, each and every day? Or are they just words you have heard a hundred times, and you still take the same unfulfilling paths, feeling frustrated in your professional life and disconnected from your true self?

In this book, you get to see the PowerTools all in one place. You'll hear from businesswomen who share their stories, rules, wisdom, and words of advice that relate to the PowerTools. You can put any of these PowerTools into practice right away and make positive changes in your business and in your life.

Sometimes, the most powerful, transformative words are the ones that you put down on paper and then say out loud. If you get the urge to read this book aloud, go for it! Sometimes, hearing other women's stories can be a light that shines on the path you know you should be taking to get beyond your obstacles but have avoided for too long. When you change course and follow your true path, you get to your real power. The path has always been there; now you can learn how to follow it without fear.

PowerTools are meant to be the stepping stones on your path.

UNDERSTANDING THE POWERTOOLS

There is no single way to experience the PowerTools, but "experience" is the operative word. By examining each PowerTool as it relates to your own life and business, you will uncover more than just thoughts and ideas for growing your business or changing aspects of your life. The PowerTools will put you in touch with the internal tactics you use—consciously or subconsciously—that either help you get through the situations you face each day or cause you to avoid them.

Most of all, the PowerTools should enable you to define what you want in your life and from your business and show you that both must be in harmony for you to be true to yourself. When your business and life are in sync, success is inevitable.

BIRTH OF THE POWERTOOLS

The PowerTools began as an impromptu speech given in 1999 to a diverse group of women at a business luncheon in Washington, DC. I gave the same speech to businesswomen in Los Angeles and then a more detailed version in Wellington, New Zealand. The reaction to the PowerTools was instantaneous and identical with each group of women, and I realized that my words were striking a universal chord.

Women's heartfelt, emotional reactions to the PowerTools convinced me that I was articulating some of the issues that many of us struggle with as we build our businesses and live our lives. As I began to speak with more women in business around the world, the PowerTools gained definition and meaning.

SHARING POWERTOOLS

The PowerTools are affirmations and advice for both your professional side and your personal side and are meant to help you not only in your business but in other aspects of your life as well.

When you think about it, men have for centuries had their own "power tools" that were often "off-limits" to women. Sure, women have had their "tools": the basket, loom, oven, typewriter. But don't you think it's about time women had some real PowerTools of their own?

And isn't it great to realize that many of our most powerful tools as women are portable because we carry them inside of ourselves? We've had them all along; we just don't often give ourselves the credit or acknowledge them. We let our inner PowerTools rust from lack of use. Don't worry—they still work!

Nearly every successful woman I have met admits that before she "found her success," she had to not only deal with life's unexpected ups and downs, but also had to face internal obstacles she had thrown in her own way. Over time, she learned to navigate a path that led to greater professional fulfillment because it was in line with her personal side. Each woman felt she was successful, even though each defined success differently.

The women in this book—some of whom I've met in person and others only through e-mail—were all open to discussing their fears and failures in addition to their successes. Many of them admitted that after telling their complete stories—not just the good parts—they gained power and strength. By helping other women, they were also helping themselves.

This book weaves together the voices and experiences of businesswomen across the country to help you find your own path and success in a way that is compatible with your life as a businesswoman and woman.

I firmly believe that because our lives as women are so intertwined with our businesses, separating them is never really an option. Because of that "inter-connectedness," we should have our own unique methods of dealing with business and life, methods that can differ greatly from men's. That's why the PowerTools exist.

HOW TO USE THIS BOOK

This book contains information in several formats. Each chapter begins with a short story of a businesswoman to demonstrate the PowerTool. Then I share some of my personal experiences and observations that helped shape the PowerTool.

Interspersed within each chapter are:

E-QUOTES — Excerpts of e-mail conversations I've had with women in business.

SHE READS—Must-read book lists with reviews written by women CEOs and presidents.

At the end of each chapter are:

NUGGETS—Additional resource lists including books, videos, and web sites to enhance your use of the PowerTools.

PERSONAL PROJECTS—Fun, unusual, or useful activities you can do or actions you can take to challenge yourself and get closer to achieving your real goals.

POWERTOOLS CHECK LIST—A bulleted list of "takeaways"— points to ponder and things to remember.

At the heart of this book are the stories of women in business who, like you and me, have multi-faceted lives and face personal and professional challenges on their way to success. Their stories are either examples of some aspect of a PowerTool or help to reinforce the PowerTool as a valid and useful strategy.

At the end of the book, you will find a list of these women, along with information about their businesses and business web sites.

Feel free to skip around or read chapters more than once. Ask your friends to join you in doing the Personal Projects. Clip out the PowerTools list and tack it onto your bulletin board or carry it in your wallet. Get online and visit the recommended sites, then e-mail them to a woman you know. Don't just read this book—experience it!

Claim the PowerTools for your own. Use them. Spread them around. Start a revolution in your business and in your life!

NOTE FROM THE AUTHOR: In this book, you will see the spelling of "web site" as two words. I personally prefer "website" as one word; however, after e-mailing the inventor of the Web, Tim Berners-Lee, I learned from his reply that he uses the two-word version. Okay, I will give in, only because one would think that the inventor of the Web must know the correct spelling of "web site."

Chapter 1

SHARE YOUR STORIES

*Teach, Inspire, Motivate, and Learn
by Telling and Listening*

"Storytelling is the oldest form of education."
—Terry Tempest Williams

ONE MINUTE, JENNIFER C. KING WAS LEADING BIOSPACE.COM, INC., a company she founded. The next minute, she was no longer in charge. After raising $14 million, the venture capitalists who invested in Jennifer's company asked her to step down as co-CEO. A month later, she was invited to speak to a group of men and women attending a motivational program.

"Sharing my personal experience with other women has been significant in my healing process after being forced to step down as CEO of the company I started 15 years ago," says Jennifer. "The experience was a major step at the beginning of my healing process. I don't know if I'll start another company or simply learn to be the best board member I can be."

Although she was still in the process of dealing with her professional setback, Jennifer acknowledged that by sharing her experiences, she was gaining just as much, if not more, than her audience. That is the power of Sharing Your Stories.

STORYTELLING AS MY CATALYST

In 1998, while attending a national women's business conference in California (Professional Business Women of California), I ran into Jenai Lane, an award-winning entrepreneur who I had met the previous year at the same event. I was interested in her business, Respect Inc., a socially responsible product innovation company located in the Bay Area, and was eager to hear how things were going for her. I also wanted to find out how her documentary film about women entrepreneurs was coming along. I admired how Jenai seemed to honor two sides of herself—the professional and creative.

At this particular conference, we decided to sit together at lunch. Our small talk quickly turned to telling stories about our businesses. I can't remember which one of us started the discussion, but we soon realized that each of us seemed to be at the exact same place with our companies. We spent the rest of lunch comparing and contrasting experiences.

We were both involved in negative business situations that were threatening our continued involvement in our companies. Because of the business woes, our personal happiness and fulfillment were at an all-time low. As we told our very painful and private professional stories, we instantly shared a bond. By the end of our conversation, we had each encouraged the other to make a major change in order to improve the situation. Both of us walked away from that lunch empowered to make the necessary changes, no matter how difficult, to get our lives back on track. Even if it meant leaving our companies.

Since Jenai and I were based on opposite coasts, we used e-mail and an occasional phone call to stay in touch and to give each other updates and pep talks. We both ended up making similar drastic changes in our professional lives, each with the underlying goal of finding inner peace, something that meant more to us than money. Jenai sold one of her brands and dissolved the rest of her business of six years, and I turned my business of five years over to my partner and embarked on a journey of personal growth in order to better understand what I should be doing professionally.

Today, Jenai has a new business—Zeal Co.—which develops innovative product ideas for companies, and she couldn't be happier. I've begun to live my lifelong dream of being a full-time writer—just a writer—and let everything else revolve around my writing instead of letting my love of writing always take a secondary position in my life.

Looking back, I realize that the very act of telling my story over lunch one day in California to another woman was a turning point. Telling my story was a tremendous relief. Almost equally important was hearing Jenai's story and getting a reassuring feeling that I was not the only woman going through a difficult and emotional time with her business. Not that I would wish a bad time on anyone else, but it was so validating to hear that someone else had been through something similar to me. Don't we all find comfort when we discover that we are not alone?

What did Jenai think of our afternoon of storytelling? "We were the token Gen Xers at that conference so we were naturally drawn to each other. The meeting that day was synchronistic. Here we were, on opposite ends of the country, thinking that we were alone in our unique situations. Surely no one our own age could possibly understand the business predicaments that we were simultaneously in. And there we were, sharing our stories and finding strength from each other.

"I believe there are no coincidences," continues Jenai. Maybe our meeting helped us to stay true to our authentic selves, to hold on to our personal vision even if that meant our company's vision might not survive. At the very least, we became friends and confidantes which has proven invaluable. As a documentary filmmaker, I believe stories heal. In some way, our meeting helped start the healing process after the death of our first companies and the birth of our new visions."

WHY TELL YOUR STORIES?

I believe firmly that women learn most readily when they hear the stories of other people's experiences. I could have started out this chapter by telling you that women's stories are valuable. I could have said how important it is to share your stories with other women. I could have observed that women often learn so much more by hearing other women's stories. But isn't it more compelling to actually read a story and be able to relate to that story than to simply have me tell you what I think?

Don't we almost automatically ignore someone who tells us what we should do? I don't think that is a "woman thing"—I think it is human nature to rebel against what others tell us to do, whether it pertains to our business or our life. Perhaps we are stubborn or convinced we know what we should be doing, even if we aren't doing it. We certainly don't want to hear what we should be doing from someone else, no matter how close they are to us or how correct their advice.

Even if we do ask for help, we often get defensive when we realize that the advice suggests we need to change something about ourselves or our situation. We might not feel comfortable changing, at least not at someone else's request. Yet if we hear a story of someone else's experience of change, we tend to listen. If we listen closely and hear the message in the story, we learn. Sometimes we are motivated to action by hearing someone else's story. Other times, we are simply motivated to tell our own stories, an act that can be just as powerful.

When we tell our stories, it is often because we think we are helping others, but more often than not, we end up helping ourselves.

SHE READS

Recommended by Kate Moon, President and Owner, Walkabout Comfort Shoe Store:

The Seat of the Soul by Gary Zukav
"In [this book], Zukav talks about 'intention.' I try hard to incorporate this into my life each day. Say I have to discipline an employee: what is my intention? Do I want to be 'the boss' and show my power, do I want to make this person a better employee, do I want to make them feel small, do I want to give them feedback in a constructive and caring way? I have the word 'intention' taped to the meeting table in my office and to the top of my computer monitor. It has really helped me to stop and think before I take action."

HONORING OUR STORIES

I mentioned in the Introduction that I've had the opportunity to travel for business and that the PowerTools came out of a speech I gave in several cities around the world. In 1999, I was invited to speak in Wellington, New Zealand. I had always dreamed of going to Australia and New Zealand but could never afford a plane ticket, so for me, the trip was a dream come true. The invitation came from the

Women's Leaders Network, a group that brought together women from around the world, particularly the Pacific Rim, to discuss the status of women globally.

A fascinating thing happened the day before I spoke. During a Q&A session after a panel discussion, a woman stood up and began to tell a story about her life. When she was finished, several other women stood up and sang a short song in unison.

I asked a woman from New Zealand what the singing meant. In the tradition of the Maori, the indigenous people of New Zealand, a song is called a waiata (why-ahrt-ah) and to stand in support of another by singing for them is to "tautoko" (tow-tor-kor). The women's song was a show of support for the woman who told her story.

How perfect! Engrained in the Maori culture is the honoring of other stories. Witnessing this custom made me realize that we all need to honor the stories of other women, but more importantly, we need to honor ourselves and our own stories. Our experiences shape our wisdom, and we pass that wisdom down through storytelling.

When a woman stands before us and shares her inner self, she is doing it to help us. We should honor her with song, praise, kindness, and support. It is only right that we thank her for her courage and generosity.

With a new appreciation for sharing stories, I realized that I had the perfect speech to give to this incredibly diverse audience of women: the Ten PowerTools. I jotted them down from memory, and as I gave my speech and told my own stories, I noticed that women were reaching into their bags for pen and paper to write down the PowerTools.

After my speech, a high priestess from a Maori tribe came up to me with tears in her eyes and held my hands in hers, thanking me for sharing my stories. I finally appreciated the power of storytelling and realized the value of my life's experiences as tools for teaching and inspiring others. I had the PowerTools.

PERSONAL PROJECT #1: LIFE STORY TITLES
CREATE TITLES FOR THE STORIES OF YOUR LIFE

When I give a speech, I always try to come up with a catchy title to represent the information and stories I am about to share. If I'm going to talk about what it was like being a woman online in the early years of the Internet, I might title my speech: "My Life and Times in Cyberspace: One Woman's Adventures Online." If I'm going to reveal what it was like being one of the first women with her own Internet company, the title might be: "Secrets of a Grrl Entrepreneur: Pioneering Woman in a Man's World."

Or if I am going to talk about women's roles and their impact on the Internet and the new media industry, I might call the speech: "The Female Invasion: How Women Are Changing the 'Net As We Know It."

In order to create a title for my life, I'd have to take a look at different aspects of my experiences or times of my life. One title would fail to capture the complexity of what I've been through. Some titles of my own life stories might be:

- "Held Up at Gunpoint: The True Story of One Woman's Journey from Fear to Empowerment." (This refers to how being held up at gunpoint changed the course of my life—see Chapter 4.)
- "Leaving It All Behind: How to Let Go of Your Business and Move On With Your Life." (This refers to how I turned my company over to my business partner and left to pursue my writing.)

- "Taking Creative Risks: Surviving Freelance Writing and Loving It." (This, of course, refers to my challenging professional path as a full-time writer.)

Creating titles for your life stories is a creative way of trying to summarize the lessons you have learned through your valuable experiences, the lessons you could teach others through your stories. Maybe you won't ever give speeches like I do, revealing pieces of your life to hundreds of total strangers each time. But knowing what you've learned and what you could teach others validates each and every one of your experiences.

Write down your Life Story Titles in your journal or print them onto colorful paper and paste them on your bathroom mirror, kitchen fridge, or computer. Write them on smaller pieces of paper and put them in your wallet. Hold onto and enjoy them.

Or better yet, write down the whole story, not just the title, and give it as a gift to your friends and family or even employees or clients, if appropriate. Honor Your Stories.

PERSONAL PROJECT #2: THE GATHERING

PLAN A GATHERING FOR STORYTELLING

When we were younger, we had so many opportunities to hang out with our friends in a nonthreatening and noncompetitive environment. We played games that "forced" us to reveal our deepest secrets and our innermost thoughts. We seemed to express ourselves without censoring our true feelings. We told our stories freely.

Now we're all grown up and chances are we're not like Carrie and her girlfriends on HBO's *Sex and the City*. We don't seem to have the time to gather with a group of friends and talk openly about our lives, even over cosmopolitans.

I highly recommend organizing a Sunday brunch with half a dozen entrepreneurial women and a pitcher of mimosas. Since this is a business book, I'm not recommending that you talk about the personal, intimate details of your life. The idea is to create a comfortable atmosphere where everyone can feel safe sharing their business experiences.

Before you begin, have everyone agree (pledge, swear) to keep everything they hear at the brunch confidential. You can even have mock "nondisclosure agreements" for everyone to sign just to get into the "no-tell" mood.

To get the conversation going, bring index cards with questions written on them that the women can pick from like a deck of cards. Here are some sample questions to get the stories flowing:

- Why did you start your business?
- What aspect of your business keeps you up at night and how do you deal with it?
- What has been your proudest moment in business?
- When was the last time your business made you cry and why?
- What is the best business advice anyone has ever given you?
- What drives you crazy about your business and what can you do about it?

You can have each woman answer her own question or have the woman who picks a question start with her story, then go around the table to get responses from the others. The key is to listen to one another and not to comment on or judge another person's story.

There is no doubt that you'll have enthusiastic requests for another brunch. Everyone will walk away from the experience feeling inspired and motivated by what they have heard, or at least feeling like they are not alone. Women in business tend to be feel isolated from others who understand what they are going through. Sometimes it requires extra effort to find the people who are having similar experiences and then take the time to share the stories.

A REAL-LIFE GATHERING OF WOMEN—"STAYING MOTIVATED"

While working on this book, I held a powerlunch at a restaurant in Portland, Maine. There were seven of us at the table, all women, all entrepreneurs, ranging in age from early 30s to late 50s.

After each question I posed we went around the table in order to give each woman an opportunity to answer. Here is an excerpt from the conversation. Note how personal information constantly blends with the professional side of the women's stories and advice.

THE WOMEN

Catherine H. Cloudman, Cloudhawk Management Consultants, LLC
MaryEllen Fitzgerald, President, Critical Insights, Inc.
Anne Kennedy, President, Beyond Ink
Christina Merrill, Head of Research, ViA, Inc.
Kate Moon, President and Owner, Walkabout Comfort Shoe Store
Anne Valentine, President/Owner, Smart Catalog

ALIZA: How do you stay motivated? (Note this opening question. Simple, leading, and loaded).

MARYELLEN: You hit cycles at different times during the season or during the day that impact you. For the most part, I don't think that I do anything special. I'm pretty competitive. This is important to me. I wake up and think "My kids and my business." Don't tell my husband. That's basically the way it goes.

ANNE V.: I'm motivated by an image, a picture I have in my mind of "this is where I want to be." This is my picture of what success looks like and it motivates me. I also have to say that I pray. I pray about all the decisions in my business. I don't look for a thunderbolt. (Laughter from the group)

Being grateful is a great motivator because you realize success has a sense of luck to it. I mean we're lucky to have our education, to have our health. Not everyone has these things. We are the lucky ones, we really are. I think everybody, even if they don't talk about it, has some degree of faith.

CHRISTINA: I look at motivation as coming from self-discipline. When I am self-disciplined, I am motivated. When I'm not self-disciplined, when I get lazy, when I'm not thinking about the best possible person I can be, I lose my motivation.

My motivation comes from two places—first from inner direct-edness and discipline. One very important component of this inner discipline is my belief in God and my relationship with everything to do with my religion. Not going overboard, but it is an absolute bottom-line piece of my inner discipline.

My outer discipline, which leads to motivation, comes from the needs of my husband and my children. They have needs which disci-pline me to remember that I may be a great businesswoman, I may be this or that, but get with it. Be a mom. Be a wife. Those are the two greatest motivators in my life.

When I'm down on the job, and I'm not being a good wife or a great mom, then the world just falls apart. And it usually happens a week before my period. (Laughter from the group.)

KATE: I think really enjoying what I do makes it easier. There are days, more lately, after 16 years [in business], when I wake up and go, "Oh, I'd love to do something else." Not that I don't want to go to Walkabout. But I am taking a little more time away which is a new thing, a new issue over the last year. But bottom line, I feel really fortunate to be doing something I like and when I'm feeling down, I say "Listen, this could be a whole lot worse, Kate."

We have a little saying at the shop when we get one of those customers who calls someone on our staff a peon, we talk about how, "Don't you just want to look at her and say the word 'Bosnia.'" You know, you're just like, "Lady, your life is a gift here, and it could be a whole lot worse."

So I guess having seen a lot of tragedy, having traveled around the world and seen a lot of sad things, I really put things into perspective. It could be a whole lot better, but it could also be a whole lot worse. I've got nothing to complain about, I really don't.

ANNE K.: There are essentially three different motivators that don't always operate at the same time. But three different things that keep me motivated. The first one is that it is essential to take care of myself. The days I don't make it to the gym, my motivation just goes like that (gesturing a downward motion), or if I don't get enough sleep. The first thing is making sure I'm taking good care of myself.

The second thing is the sense of having a good time, of really enjoying what I'm doing.

The other thing is when I look at my bank balance. I put three kids through private college, and I have some big loans, and the whole point of this business, besides making a contribution to this world, is to get out of debt so I can sit back and write the novels that don't sell.

My bank balance is a powerful motivator and the corollary to that is making the payroll.

CATHERINE: Interestingly enough, I work with lots of business owners designing incentive compensation programs to help motivate their people. While there is no question that the money factor helps— if I am real honest with myself it is not what motivates me personally. Let me try to answer this in a couple of ways.

First—I love to learn. The harder the challenge, the harder I work. I love to tackle new issues, and I am a bulldog about getting to the right or best answer through research, critical thinking, and creativity.

Second—I am the most motivated when I am very busy. I have been this way since I was a kid. I got the best grades in school when I was working a few jobs and involved in a lot of extracurricular activities.

Third—I live by deadlines, whether self-imposed or provided to me. I hate to miss a deadline, and I can't really think of a time when I have. My partner tells me I have an urgency addiction!

Finally—I am probably more competitive than I let on. I like to do the best work possible and part of judging whether or not something is at its "best" is comparing it to alternatives.

A FEW DAYS LATER

These diverse stories, experiences, and words of advice came from a single two-hour lunch. The day after our conversation, Anne Kennedy came up to me at a networking event and thanked me for organizing the lunch and leading the conversation. She said she hadn't always taken the time to get together with other women entrepreneurs. She felt so invigorated and motivated after hearing the stories of other women in business. That is the Power of Stories.

A FEW MONTHS LATER

An e-mail I received from Christina Merrill let me know that, inspired by the gathering, some women in Portland, Maine, have started a group called La Femme (Female Executives Making It in Maine) that is geared toward both executive women and women business owners. The power of one gathering continues to affect these women's lives in positive ways.

POWERTOOL 1 CHECKLIST
Share Your Stories

- *Be honest about where you have been and what you have learned and share your experiences with other people.*
- *Don't leave out your mistakes and foibles when you tell your stories because those are where the most powerful lessons are learned.*
- *Honor other women's stories. When a woman has the courage to stand up and talk about her life, thank her for it.*
- *Buy and read books about women's stories, then pass them on to other women you know.*
- *Consider writing your own story, either for yourself, to publish on the Web, or as a book.*

NUGGETS

BOOKS OF WOMEN'S STORIES

American Women's Autobiography: Feasts of Memory, Margo Culley, ed.,
Wisconsin Press, 1992

*In Her Own Words : Women's Memoirs from Australia, New Zealand, Canada
and the United States*, Jill Ker Conway, ed., Vintage Books, 1999

A Sounding of Women: Autobiographies from Unexpected Places, Martha C.
Ward, ed., Allyn and Bacon, 1997

*Writing Women's Lives: An Anthology of Autobiographical Narratives by 20th
Century American Women Writers*, Susan Cahill, ed., Harper Perennial,
1994

*Written by Herself : Women's Memoirs from Britain, Africa, Asia, and the United
States*, Jill Ker Conway, ed., Vintage Books, 1996

Written by Herself : Autobiographies of American Women : An Anthology, Jill
Ker Conway, ed., Vintage Books, 1992

BOOKS ON WRITING YOUR LIFE STORY

Living to Tell the Tale: A Guide to the Writing Memoir, Jane Taylor McDonnell,
Penguin USA, 1998

Writing the Memoir: From Truth to Art, Judith Barrington, Eighth Mountain Press, 1997

*Your Life as Story: Discovering the "New Autobiography" and Writing Memoir
as Literature*, Tristine Rainer, JP Tarcher, 1998

WEB SITES ABOUT HERSTORY

We Have Lived Important Lives—List of women's biographies
www.lib.ttu.edu/womens_studies/WOMBIO.htm

American Literature
www.library.wisc.edu/libraries/WomensStudies/core/cramlit.htm

The World Wide Web Virtual Library/Women's History
wwwliisg.nl/~womhist/vlwhalph.html

Women's Studies Resources on the WWW
duncan.cup.edu/~hartman/wsres1.htm

Women's History
womenshistory.about.com/

Women of Achievement and Herstory
www.undelete.org/woa.html

Chapter 2

TAKE CHARGE OF CHANGE

*Make Change Happen Rather Than
Letting It Run Your Life and Business*

*"If you had to choose only two qualities to get you through times of change,
the first should be a sense of self-worth and the second a sense of humor."*

—**Jennifer James**

WHO COULD IMAGINE THAT EBAY WOULD BRING HEATHER DUKE, president of Profoundia, closer to her professional dream? After an unsuccessful first career as a teacher in a private alternative school, Heather Duke was on unemployment, discouraged, and filled with self-doubt. To make ends meet, she began selling used books on eBay. After much research, she decided to sell a product online and chose bindis, a form of Indian body adornment. She and her husband joined forces to build an e-commerce web site.

From employment to unemployment to self-employment, Heather was forced to adapt to change, which made her stronger. "Building Profoundia restored my confidence in myself. I had help from my husband, John, but what I realized is that the resources exist for me to do this on my own," says Heather.

The best kind of change is the change that you initiate for a purpose instead of the change that hits you when you least expect it. If change does happen, you should make it work for you.

CHANGE IN MY OWN LIFE

Many of us live life allowing changes to happen to us while others look at changes as the fuel that makes things happen. Personally, I've always tended to take the act of making changes to an extreme. I reacted to the changes in my early life by becoming a change-a-holic. I point to my Navy-brat upbringing as the catalyst for this turbo-change behavior. My family moved everytime my Dad got stationed in a new place. Every two years or so, we'd pack our things and leave behind the people and places that had just started to become familiar. I was forced to adapt to being uprooted and changing locations every other year.

The effects of moving around as a child began to manifest in college, or rather, at three different colleges. First was the college for fashion merchandising because I couldn't think of anything else to do. Next came a transfer to the University of Virginia to pursue a more liberal arts curriculum, but after a year, I moved to Richmond, Virginia, and took classes at a local university.

Finally, I left college and started to work. But that was only the beginning of my turbo-change lifestyle. Over the last ten years, I've had four distinct careers: in the music business, running a nonprofit organization on domestic violence awareness, starting an Internet company called Cybergrrl, Inc., and now full-time writer. That is a lot of career changing in a short amount of time.

Even my living arrangements were affected by a need to constantly change. In my first five years in New York City, I moved to a dozen different apartments in various neighborhoods throughout Manhattan, choosing apartments with short subleases or short-term leases. You can only imagine the number of times I rearranged the furniture in each apartment to satisfy this need to change.

Does this need for constant change sound familiar to you? Or does change scare you? Some women I've spoken with say they will never initiate change. However, they do admit to being able to adapt when change happens to them. They deal with change out of sheer necessity.

There are probably a lot of women like me, who have created both chaotic and smooth changes in their lives for no apparent reason, with or without a plan. Changing has been a way to find my true path, but ironically, most of the changes I created were not direct lines to my ultimate goals because I wasn't paying attention to my heart.

CHANGE HAPPENING TO YOU

If you have ever experienced a major setback after following through on a plan, there are basically two ways you can respond: retreat and claim defeat, or push forward and take charge of the unexpected change, seeing it as an opportunity instead of a setback.

Let's meet some women who harnessed the unexpected changes in their lives and moved forward despite—or because of—those changes.

Brenda K. Stier, now president of Marketing Works, Inc., has built two businesses: one out of a situation where change happened to her, and the other when she was in a situation that she knew she had to change.

While she was working as a public relations coordinator for a small ad agency, the firm experienced financial difficulties and closed without any warning. She was in the middle of projects with several clients and out of a deep feeling of responsibility, Brenda offered to finish those projects and let the clients pay her directly. Soon, more work and referrals came in, and what was initially a temporary situation became Brenda's full-time business.

When one of her clients offered her office space within his building, Brenda immediately moved a computer into a cubicle there. When another client called shortly after, asking to whom they should make out a check for payment, Brenda looked out the window at the street sign—Greencrest Drive—and replied, "Greencrest Marketing." She operated Greencrest Marketing for three years as a sole proprietorship, then incorporated the business and added a partner as a 50 percent shareholder in the corporation.

Over the next five years, Brenda's business grew. However, it also became apparent to her that she and her partner had very different views on business, relationships, and life in general. "I not only hated getting up every morning and going into work, I became embarrassed to be associated with the company," Brenda admits.

She wanted out and offered to leave the company and take only the clients that wanted to leave with her. Unfortunately, she and her partner could not agree on a fair business valuation for the partner to buy Brenda's shares in the company. The dispute turned into a lawsuit. Nearly a year later, the dissolution of her business partnership was finally resolved through mediation.

Again, Brenda felt obligated to take care of her existing clients so she moved her business into her home and began operating as a consultant . Today, five years later, Marketing Works, Inc., functions as an outsourced marketing department and has grown from Brenda's home into a 2,000 square-foot facility with six employees.

Looking back at the changes in her professional life, Brenda says, "I was raised by parents who started and ended their careers with the same employer. I am a very loyal person, and if circumstances had been different, I probably would have worked for the same firm my entire life. With each major change, you think it's the end of the world, only to look back and realize it was the most positive, life-altering change that could have ever happened. You learn the most from the difficult experiences. And it's those experiences that you'll also never forget."

Brenda went through career changes first initiated by the action of others, but she held on to what she believed in to move past what could have been setbacks and instead, created new opportunity. Now she can run her business in a way that is compatible with her own values, and can honor the sense of responsibility and caring she feels for her clients, a quality that led to starting her own business in the first place.

DISCOVERING WHAT TO CHANGE

Do you change yourself for the approval of others? Are you doing what you're doing professionally because you think it is what is expected of you? Are you doing what you think you want to be doing, but deep down inside, you know that you are not? Rachel Alexander's career as a professional athlete took several unexpected turns as she got in touch with what she really wanted out of life.

Rachel Alexander spent eight years becoming a champion hang-glider pilot, achieved enormous success, and then gave it all up to follow her real dream.

At 19, Rachel set her sights on becoming a champion hang glider and making the New Zealand world team. Even today, hang gliding is a male-dominated sport with women representing only 5 percent of all pilots. To achieve her goal, Rachel gave up her marketing career, her friends, money, men, and her normal routines to go overseas and fly full-time around Europe.

After eight years of determination, focus, sacrifice, and emotional struggle, Rachel finally achieved her goals. She had become a professional hang-glider pilot, represented New Zealand three times at world hang-gliding championships, was fully-sponsored to attend world events several times, and qualified for the New Zealand team for the OPEN class worlds.

Getting into the OPEN class worlds was one of the greatest aspects of her achievements since they were separate from the women's worlds and had been dominated by men for the past 15 years. In 1995, Rachel was one of only two women out of 200 athletes to compete at the World Hang Gliding Champs in Spain.

Rachel admits that while reaching her goals was a fantastic achievement and she was even dubbed the "adventure queen" of New Zealand, she didn't feel great about her accomplishments. She had achieved her goals and become a role model for women in extreme sports, but did not feel passionate about what she was doing.

Explains Rachel, "Looking back, I had purposely chosen a sport I was not good at and set a goal to see if people at the top really are 'naturals' or if they just work harder than everyone else, which was my hypothesis. I discovered they just want it more than other people and are prepared to put up with more sacrifices to get there. Now I had arrived there, and I realized it wasn't hang gliding that I loved. I was merely proving a hypothesis."

In search of her true direction, she turned to a friend of hers who was a champion triathlete and asked him if he really loved triathlons. He gave her a poem which came from the package of an Australian cereal, Hubbards. The poem was called "The Apricot."

> *You should learn that you can't be loved by everyone.*
> *You may be the finest apricot in the world, succulent, juicy, huge*
> *   and tasty,*

Offering yourself to all, but there will be some people who do not like apricots.

You must understand that if you are the world's finest apricot and someone that you like doesn't happen to like apricots, then you have the choice of acting like a banana.

But you must be warned that if you become like a banana, there will always be people that do not like bananas.

Furthermore, you could spend your entire life trying to be the best banana, which is impossible because you are an apricot!

Or you can seek again to be the best apricot.

Contemplating the meaning of the poem, Rachel soon realized that hang gliding was her "banana" and that, ever since childhood, she had loved horses, something her parents were sure she'd outgrow. Rachel knew that horses were her "apricot." After seeing a game of polo and loving it, she sat down to write a list of all of her hang-gliding gear, put everything up for sale, and enrolled in her first horseback riding lesson.

Four years later, Rachel is about to begin her first season at polo.

As if Rachel's major change from one challenging sport to another was not enough, she also applied her theories about "apricots and bananas" to other aspects of her professional life, vowing to make a living on her own terms. She knew that working for someone else was also a "banana," so she set herself a goal to leave her day job as a tourism and marketing consultant for KPMG and set up her own business. Nearly three years after she left her job, she has a thriving advertising agency with six people on staff.

Says Rachel, "The moral of the story is: spend some time working out what are your bananas, then have the courage to ditch them and chase apricots!" As Rachel showed, identifying what you love ver-sus what you think you should love or be doing is the beginning of moving toward getting the things you want, both in your professional life and your personal life.

Rachel's story proves that the more you take the time to get to know yourself and understand your likes and dislikes, the quicker you'll get to the heart of what you want to do and where you want to be. When you can finally see what you really want to be doing from your own point of view, not through the eyes of others, you will be able to more clearly define the changes you need to make to align your work with your life.

MAKING CHANGE HAPPEN

The catalyst for becoming your own personal "change agent," that is, orchestrating the changes in your life, differs for each one of us. Making change often comes out of a need to be true to yourself, to recognize and do away with negative situations that cause you to com-promise. Perhaps it is an undeniable instinct for self-preservation that instigates change. Regardless of the reason, making change happen can take place at various stages of your professional career or your life, and it is up to you to be at the helm of that change.

For Mary Azzarto, CEO of Plumb Design, Inc., seeing change in a positive light has been a personal goal throughout her career. Each time she lives through a major professional transition, from a new job to a promotion to a relocation, she tries to see the shift as a challenge to reconfirm what is important to her and to move forward in a direc-tion that is true to her personal values.

When she was 23 years old, Mary worked for a consultant as an analyst. Her responsibilities included initiating a quarterly newsletter, and she assembled a team to produce the newsletter and even worked after-hours for a month to write, edit, and design a prototype. After presenting the sample newsletter to her boss, he gave her the go-ahead to publish the first issue. The newsletter she had created received rave reviews. Then suddenly, her boss not only withdrew his support of the project, but screamed at her during a team meeting to announce, in no uncertain terms but without a reason, that he was putting a stop to the newsletter.

After her attempt to talk to her boss privately about his decision to pull the plug on the newsletter failed, Mary realized that her boss felt threatened by her ideas and the success of the newsletter. She left her job shortly after that realization, and looked for opportunities where she could put her intelligence, initiative, and experience to better use.

Mary could have chosen to remain in her position. She could have tried to change her boss's resistance to her ideas. Or she could have accepted defeat and made sure she did not to attract attention to herself. Instead, she concluded she would be wasting energy that she could use to build her professional skills and serve customers. She knew that she could not afford to stay in a job where her talents and ideas were not only underutilized, but actively being suppressed.

Leaving her job wasn't easy for Mary, but in hindsight, she says it turned out to be the right decision. It taught her not to sell herself short and to see "opportunity in adversity," which led her to start her own business.

Says Mary, "I think many women are initially intimidated by change, but it only takes one turn for the positive to realize that being stagnant works against you, both personally and professionally. One challenge [women face] is that many women are brought up to be 'fixers,' and therefore will stay in a bad situation—one that might even be harmful to them—and try to fix it, even when fixing it is neither in their best interest nor within their power."

Mary feels another challenge for women is unlearning the fear and intimidation that has been "taught" to them over the years by people in power positions—such as their bosses—who do not want to hear their ideas or watch them succeed. She believes women can benefit from having an "I can do anything" attitude.

To women who are afraid to change, Mary says don't wait for someone else to improve your life, either at home or work. It is up to you to take responsibility, "grab the reins and harness change to your advantage." The inevitable bumps in the road that you encounter will teach you more about yourself, particularly your adaptability, capabilities, and strength.

Katherine Weldon, CEO of eTime Solutions, Inc., cites three specific times when she initiated major change in her life despite less-than-ideal circumstances. The first was when she returned to school, at the age of 28 and as a single mother of two, to finish her degree and then started her own 3-D animation company. The second was at 35 when she decided to join an Internet start-up, accepting stock as payment, at a time when she had no other financial resources. The third major change was when she decided to start eTime Solutions, Inc., her second company.

To get to the point of owning her own Internet company, Katherine took a rather long and circuitous path. While a teenager, she had her first daughter and left home soon after to get married. She was able to get her G.E.D. in time for high school graduation, then enrolled in a community college, taking classes with the thought of becoming a doctor.

Two years after her first daughter was born, she and her high school sweetheart separated, then divorced. She took a job at a psychiatric medical center while going to school. There she met a resident psychiatrist, fell in love, and married again. She continued going to school for a while during her second pregnancy.

At that time, a woman approached Katherine, asking her if she had ever considered modeling. Admits Katherine, "I figured that if I was still asked that question when I was eight months pregnant that maybe I should check in to it. I thought this might be a flexible way to earn additional income, and it would be fun." After her daughter was born, Katherine went to visit an agent, took classes, and started working as a model right away. At the time, she thought she could always go back to school but would not always be able to be a model.

Her husband finished his residency, and Katherine encouraged him to start a private practice in psychiatry. While helping him set up software to manage the business, she became comfortable with computers.

Then, her mother died suddenly, forcing Katherine to reevaluate her own life by looking at her mother's life. Her mother, Katherine felt, lived by the idea that "you grow up, marry a 'catch,' define yourself as a Wife and Mother, sacrifice your needs for the good of everyone else, be a good girl, and you will be rewarded." But Katherine had witnessed that the fairy tale didn't pan out for her mother.

For a long time, Katherine coped with her mother's death by becoming her mother's complete mirror image, diving into her modeling career, traveling everywhere, and using the whirlwind of activity as a way to bury her grief.

In 1988, Katherine resurfaced after six years of grieving. "I realized I was to be 30 in another year, and I wasn't the person I wanted be.

The change was rather dramatic. I reflected for awhile and then decided what I needed to do. I got a divorce, because I had been avoiding the fact that the years of turmoil had taken a toll on my marriage, and we could not revive it. I also wanted to go back to school. Once in school, I was back on track, and I instantly knew it."

Katherine pursued a degree in film production with a concentration of study in 3-D animation, graduated *cum laude* after two and a half years, then used money she had inherited from her mother's estate to purchase 3-D equipment and started a business from home. A few years later, her company merged with another. However, Katherine had learned that the costs of high-end animation were high and the returns were low. She had to make another change sooner than later if she was going to survive financially.

In 1994, Katherine's brother suggested she look into the Internet for a possible career move. She joined a new media company in its early stages, taking stock instead of a big salary, which was a major financial risk, but she knew she had found the ideal medium for her interests. The company she was working to grow was eventually sold. Despite an offer from her employer of a major raise and promotion to vice president of the company, Katherine resigned because she disagreed with the way the new leadership was running the business. Soon after her departure, she and another employee at the same new media company joined forces to start eTime Solutions, Inc., to develop web-based applications.

Says Katherine, "What I have observed in my own family and friends is that women generally are very reluctant to change. I think we are conditioned to believe that if we sacrifice our needs for the good of the family, we will somehow be rewarded in the end. But I think that is an outdated concept and many women have been terribly disappointed."

By realizing she was different from her mother, Katherine learned to accept the fact that she did things in her own way and that doing so was OK. Currently, Katherine lives on a sailboat and plans to sail around the world for her next big adventure. "I want to keep experiencing new things until it's my time to go, and even then, I hope they have to ship me home from another country."

Change happens. Change is inevitable. Both Mary and Katherine acknowledge that change can be difficult, even frightening, but both pushed beyond doubts and fears to create businesses they love. Change was essential in moving them forward.

You can either allow change to happen to you and be buffeted around by events "beyond your control," or you can assess the situation and make the changes work in your favor or create additional changes to move your life forward in the direction that feels right to you.

Always be open to change. Being open to change helps you to create opportunities, even when the changes aren't planned.

PERSONAL PROJECT #1:

DEPLOY THE MINI-CHANGE AGENT

Sometimes the smallest change can have the greatest impact. What can you do today within your business—a small change—that could have a big effect?

Often, as we run our businesses, we forget the little things that can make a big difference in the corporate culture of our companies. By changing a policy or implementing a new program, you can infuse life and your own spirit back into the business.

Here are some Mini-Change Agents to deploy in your business to bring about ripples of positive change:

- Plan a monthly field trip for staff that allows the group to bond away from the office while being exposed to something you feel they should know about. Or bring in a speaker once a month to present an interesting concept to your team.

- Introduce flex-time or telecommuting. If you aren't creating flexibility for your own worklife, chances are you aren't creating it for others on your team. Come up with a clear plan for allowing your staff a degree of flexibility and then take advantage of it yourself as well. Set a positive example and enjoy the benefits of this policy change.

- Create a Never-Miss Meeting. Not all meetings have to be about day-to-day business. Have a weekly or biweekly meeting where the goal is exploration and discovery—like a grown-up version of Show and Tell. Tap into the personal interests of your team. Use articles in a magazine like *Fast Company* as a catalyst for creative discussion.

When you started your own business, weren't you looking forward to creating a business that felt right to you? When the "you" gets lost in day-to-day operations, try to get back in touch with what you wanted to build in the first place, then take steps to get back to that point. One change at a time.

PERSONAL PROJECT #2:
THE PLACEMENT OF THINGS

What can you do to change your physical environment to increase productivity, profitability, or your overall sense of well-being? The Chinese believe that the placement, shape, and color of structures and objects can have a powerful impact on your life, your energy, and the ch'I—or the positive energy—around you. In response to this belief, they developed Feng Shui (pronounced Fung SHWAY), the Chinese Art of Placement.

Here are a few Feng Shui tips to implement right away for positive change in your workspace:

- Reposition your desk so that you are facing in the direction of the entrance into the room. If you can't move the furniture in that way but you are working at your computer with your back to the doorway, hang a convex mirror on the wall in front of you or attach it to your computer so you can see behind you. The idea is to keep you from being surprised.
- If you do not have windows for a view of the outdoors, hang photographs of nature scenes on the wall. Or put a potted plant next to your computer. Create something pleasing to the eye and soul.
- If you can't open a window for circulation, buy a small fan and position it near a plant to create a rustling of leaves. The movement and sound will help you feel more energetic.
- If a tall piece of furniture is visible in the room where you are working, move it out of your line of sight. Otherwise, you may feel a reduced sense of well-being and adequacy.
- Sharp angles can be unlucky in an office. Strategically place plants at corners of furniture or in corners where walls meet to soften the edges.

Understanding that your environment can have a major effect on not only your comfort but also your attitude and health is a starting point for creating change around you. Changing small things to improve your surroundings can bring about immediate and positive results.

POWERTOOL 2 CHECKLIST
Be Open to Change

- *When change happens to you, take advantage of it and don't let it take control of you.*
- *Make change happen in your life by examining what should change and then taking the steps to make that change.*
- *Don't be afraid to jump into change and figure it out later.*
- *Sometimes the smallest changes can lead to enormous transformations.*

NUGGETS

BOOKS ON FENG SHUI

Clear Your Clutter with Feng Shui, Karen Kingston, Broadway Books, 1999
Feng Shui Goes to the Office: How to Thrive from 9 to 5, Nanilee Wydra, Contemporary Books, 2000
Lillian Too's Easy-to-Use Feng Shui, Lillian Too, Sterling Publications, 1999
Move Your Stuff, Change Your Life: How to Use Feng Shui to Get Love, Money, Respect and Happiness, Karen Rauch Carter; Fireside, 2000
The Western Guide to Feng Shui: Room by Room, Terah Kathryn Collins, Hay House, 1999

WEB SITES ON FENG SHUI

About.com's Chinese Culture
 chineseculture.about.com/culture/chineseculture/cs/fengshui
Geomancy.net
 www.geomancy.net
SpiritWeb: Feng Shui
 www.spiritweb.org/Spirit/feng-shui.html
AllFengShui.com
 www.alfengshui.com

Chapter 3

NEVER STOP LEARNING

It's Never Too Late to Discover Something New

*"Never mistake knowledge for wisdom. One helps you make a living,
the other helps you make a life."*

—Sandra Carey

HARON GOLDMACHER, PRESIDENT OF COMMUNICATIONS 21, INC., enrolled in a nine-month business leadership development program. With the kick-off retreat and first course, she was learning not only new ways to run her business, but also about herself.

"I think what I've learned so far is that life is short, and you have to learn to stop and smell the roses. It sounds corny but it's true," says Sharon. "I can't believe I started my business eight years ago—it has flown by—and if I'm not careful, another eight will go by without taking vacations or making time to do the things I love."

Through her courses, Sharon has also learned that a courageous leader isn't one that does or knows it all, but instead empowers and trusts the people around them to do what they do best. She is now making a more conscious effort to give her team the tools they need to take initiative and run with their own ideas. It is never too late to learn!

LEARNING MY WAY

For many of us, formal learning ends after we leave school. Whether it is lack of time, money, or motivation, or due to other extenuating circumstances, returning to school or taking classes isn't usually an option, or so we think. For a society that places so much emphasis on schooling and academic degrees, we tend to take for granted the incredible process of learning.

As already mentioned, my own educational process was eclectic, to say the least, without a focus on any single major. I simply took whatever classes sounded interesting. Two years away from several possible degrees and in my fourth year of college, I decided to leave and try learning on the job.

I've come to accept that I'm a nontraditional learner and respond better to learning experiences outside of the traditional classroom—at work, a workshop or seminar, from hearing another woman's story, or through reading a book or magazine. Often, the best learning results from just doing something—the "sink-or-swim" method—and some of the most lasting lessons come through making mistakes.

Some of your most powerful learning experiences happen when you learn about yourself, uncover your weaknesses, and then face them head-on, regardless of the consequences.

The process of learning—either by traditional or nontraditional means—is an essential part of taking charge of change as discussed in the previous chapter. Many of the women who took an active role in the changes occurring in their lives were also in "turbo-learning" mode—they had to be in order to tackle new and unforeseen events. See what you can uncover about your own way of learning by hearing how other women learn.

THE VALUE OF TRADITIONAL LEARNING

Have you made time to take courses or return to school? Returning to a "traditional" path of learning can be challenging, yet incredibly rewarding. You often gain confidence in business and in yourself after completing a course and learning a new skill.

While working as a customer service representative, Chris O'Brien decided to go back to school at night and get her college degree. Her original motivation was to be a good role model for her two-year-old son—she thought his mother should be a college graduate. Once in school, Chris began to feel motivated to further her education for herself. She was discovering her talents and could finally embark on a business that embodied her true self.

Initially, Chris was able to get her employer to cover school tuition when she pursued a general business degree. Over time, however, Chris realized that she had a talent for both writing and creative design, and with the encouragement of a professor, she transferred to another college and switched majors to a communications program. She made the decision to pursue her own interests and cultivate her talents, even though her employer would no longer pay for tuition. She soon quit her job and started her own business, DesignWrite Presentations.

In addition to learning graphic design, Web design, and writing skills in school, she also learned to trust her instincts when dealing with business clients. "I used to check to see how other designers approached projects, or how other writers set up their copy," explains Chris. "Now I try not to do that. When I present clients with something totally original, with a fresh approach—my approach—I find they're happier."

After five years, Chris is finally graduating and looking forward to growing her company. She encourages everyone to go back to school and feels that the experience truly changed her life.

Pauline Lally took over her father's company, Piping Systems, Inc., in 1993, creating a non-stop learning situation. For her, learning means combining traditional course-taking with working with a personal coach, something she has done for the last several years. Each week, she speaks with her coach during a one-hour conference call and is given assignments that she and her staff have to complete.

Since working with a coach, Pauline has implemented several systems in her company, including project management, lead generation, financial management, and identifying and acting on key frustrations. She believes coaching has also enabled her to do more long-range planning and put strategies in place for others to run the company when she no longer wants to. Overall, the learning she has done with her coach has made her more confident and proactive than ever.

But Pauline's learning methods don't stop there. She already holds a B.S. in accounting yet knows she needs technical expertise to keep up with the rapid changes in her industry. She is therefore studying for her pipefitters license and working to become certified as a women business enterprise.

In addition to going to trade school, Pauline is also pursuing an associate's degree in mechanical engineering at her local community college. The two-year program will take her longer since she can only attend part-time, but she is not deterred. She is already planning to take two four-day project management courses in 2001.

Along the way, Pauline took courses at the E-Myth Academy in California, a learning facility inspired by the book *The E-Myth Revisited: Why Most Small Businesses Don't Work and What to Do About It* by Michael Gerber. She has also taken Dale Carnegie courses that have helped her to better relate to her employees and become a more effective manager.

"I learn by keeping my ears and mind open all the time. I listen and take a lot of notes. I believe I have an advantage in a male-dominated field," says Pauline. "Often men would like to ask questions, but don't because they are afraid others will think they are naïve or stupid. No one seems to mind if a woman asks questions, and I ask a lot of them. The key to learning is listening."

There are so many different schools you can attend and courses you can take, part time, full time, and even online (see the list of web-based courses at the end of this chapter). Study at your own pace and gain knowledge and skills that can help you grow as a businesswoman, a leader, and a person.

NONTRADITIONAL LEARNING

By combining traditional learning methods with the less traditional ones, you can re-energize forgotten parts of your brain, tapping into wells of creativity that have stagnated from inactivity and revitalizing old ways of thinking. Here are some women who have chosen less obvious methods of learning to reach their business and life goals.

Sometimes, taking a course in a topic totally unrelated to your industry can bring about valuable learning. After over 22 years in the text and reference book publishing industry, Beth Lewis made a dramatic career change. She purchased Computer Coach, Inc., from the father/son team that founded it, then transformed it from an adult learning center to a school licensed by the state of Florida.

Beth learned a lot about business as she reshaped her new company, but in terms of learning, she hasn't stopped at the specific needs of her company. For her own enjoyment and growth, she attends workshops and classes on a wide range of subjects, from venture capital to history of the Bible to mastering various software programs.

"I am steeped in education all day, every day, with running a computer and technical school," explains Beth. "But since I don't want to become one-dimensional, I find that taking classes that are not always

---

E-QUOTE: SHERRY HARSCH-PORTER, PRESIDENT, PORTER BAY GROUP

"The best word to describe my learning and development style is 'holistic.' I believe strongly in traditional education coupled with experiential and nontraditional learning. I completed my Master's, took coursework toward a Ph.D., and completed two professional certifications while pursuing my career in large corporations. When I made the decision to become an entrepreneur, I began to explore ways to stimulate my creativity. In the last three years, I have attended several personal development seminars, begun learning the violin, experimented with dream journaling, and begun studying yoga. I'm beginning a painting course next month with a local artist and plan to take a personal essay writing course after the first of the year. Taken together, these experiences not only enrich my life—they inform and enrich my work. I cannot imagine learning in any other way."

---

directly computer- and business-related helps me keep my mind open, helps me think creatively and focus on something outside of the day-to-day dilemmas related to being an entrepreneur."

Taking classes ranging from belly dancing to ceramics to cardio-kickboxing creates both learning opportunities and an energy outlet for Tamara Remedios, President and owner, Xplore Communications.

When she first started her marketing business, Tamara felt as if the lines between her personal and business lives had become blurred. Out of the blue, she decided to take a class at a local community school, and not one related to her work. Her first class was belly dancing which met once a week for six weeks, a short time commitment that suited her busy schedule.

Her weekly break soon became "addictive," and she found herself signing up for more classes. In addition to relieving stress, her classes were a chance to not have to concentrate on business and let her mind wander.

"It is time I set aside each week or month to do something other than work, which is often difficult in a one-woman business. This wandering time is probably the best thing for a creative person because that is when the best ideas come to you," says Tamara. "Soon after my class or weekly break, I find myself writing down tons of ideas and flighty thoughts that were in my head. It's also great to know that I am still learning and expanding my mind, and what I'm learning usually makes a great conversation topic with new or existing clients."

LEARNING BY DOING

For some women, the "sink-or-swim" method of learning works just fine. Often, some of our best lessons, though difficult, are the ones learned right on the job, by "just doing it."

For Christine Harmel, CEO of The Interactive Resource, launching a business alone, in a new city, was her version of throwing herself into the deep end of the pool. Armed with a good idea and some guts, Christine set out to build her business, learning everything she could as she went. Today she calls herself a "digital yenta" because her new media business offers matchmaking services to help clients find Web resources such as people, office space, venture money, mergers and acquisitions, partners, and Web development agencies.

One example of how Christine had to learn by doing was when a well-known technology company asked her to assist them with mergers and acquisitions after the one deal they had initiated didn't work out well. When they called her, Christine didn't know how to price her knowledge and experience. Nor did she know how to negotiate a deal with the firm to get a fair price for tapping into all of her research and connections.

Christine admits that in her line of business, bringing together relationships is not always quantifiable. She did some fast learning by calling up several people she knew for advice and gathering as much data as possible to make her best guess. Then the client wanted to negotiate her down in price. After talking with additional advisors and friends, Christine realized that her services were extremely valuable to the client. Despite her fear that she would lose the entire deal by being stubborn, she stood her ground and insisted on the original price she had quoted.

"Not only did I learn how to hardball a negotiation, but my own confidence in the value of my knowledge was boosted," says Christine. "If they didn't want to work with me because of price, then they could go ahead and do their own mergers and acquisitions and see how it turned out!"

Being willing to learn on the job and on her own is what led Caryn Cameron, owner of Praxis Consulting, from secretarial work to starting her own part-time Web design business. While working as a secretary, she took advantage of a temporary lull in the workload to begin designing a web site for a special project at her company.

By reading books, referring to the Hypertext Markup Language (HTML) source code on other Web pages, and taking an occasional three-hour overview class of Web design, Caryn was able to acquire the skills needed to complete the web site. Her bosses liked the initial site, and when the project ended, she redesigned her company's own web site. When a contract position became available for a full-time designer at her company, Caryn didn't feel she had all the technical expertise required. She went for the job anyway, and got it.

By volunteering her Web skills for a nonprofit organization, Caryn is constantly practicing her HTML and design skills. She uses online resources such as WebMonkey.com to learn technical information and reads Web development books by designers such as Molly Holzschlag and Laura LeMay to hone her skills and keep up with the ever-changing technology. Recently, Caryn started her own part-time web design business working with a few clients under the name Praxis Consulting.

"Being willing to learn on my own got me here, along with the generosity of the many people who shared their knowledge and the bosses who let me try," says Caryn. "When I look back, my life plan wasn't well-focused, but learning new things at each step gave me the skills [I needed] to take the next step."

Christine and Caryn took the initiative to put themselves in positions where they had to learn on the job, a strategy that proved successful for them both.

LEARNING ABOUT YOURSELF

There are so many ways to learn, as you've just seen, but sometimes our greatest lessons may be much less tangible than learning a new skill. Learning about yourself—coming to a revelation or an understanding about who you are and what you want out of life—is the best kind of learning you can do. If you are attentive, you can learn more about yourself during the various events that happen as you live your life. Even as you go through traditional learning situations, self-discovery is inevitably part of the experience.

Here are several women whose greatest lessons were those where they were forced—or they forced themselves—to look inside themselves.

A journey of self-discovery led Carmen Matthews, owner, director, and Autonomous Fem Coach of Serene Samurai, to start her company and coin her professional title to best describe her mission. She became an "Autonomous Fem Coach," which she defines as someone who "guides women, ages 14 to 60, to find their own wisdom." Carmen felt the need to create an identity that told the world she was serious about making a difference in how women see themselves.

After 12 years in the Army, Carmen had realized that her résumé—which only described her expertise in computer technologies and related work experience—didn't match what she was born to do, which was to teach others to live more fully. She purchased personal development packages from late-night infomercials, including Anthony Robbins' *30 Days to Unlimited Power*, and studied the lessons, writing down thoughts about her relationship with her mother, an issue she felt was key to what was keeping her from "being her best self."

Carmen wrote over 3,000 documents and hundreds of journals about her life and self-exploration, and when she felt she had no more need to write about the past, she started her own company. Today she is a public speaker, mother/daughter coach, advice columnist, publisher of a subscription newsletter, and "Autonomous Fem Coach," combining her written words, a linguistics degree, and even her Army experiences into a mission to guide women and girls to "earn trust in themselves."

According to Nancy Ging, the owner of Turtle Island Web Design, she is probably on her 38th career. She has done everything from squeezing roe out of five-day-dead herring to journalism to middle management within a corporation to working as a psychologist in community mental health centers to building a private counseling practice to brokering commercial fishing vessels to starting an alternative bookstore. Most recently, Nancy taught herself Web design skills and has started a new home business, Turtle Island Web Design. Her projected annual revenues will be in the six figures.

Nancy recounts a powerful childhood lesson that has helped her face many challenges throughout her adult life. When she was a little girl, she used to spend summers at her grandfather's iron mining operation. Sometimes he would take her in a four-wheel drive vehicle through the Nevada desert to look at other mining claims. Since they were off-road and miles from anywhere, her grandfather allowed Nancy to drive from the time she was eight years old, reasoning that if anything ever happened to him, she should be able to drive to get help.

On one particular day, they were driving the boundaries of a group of claims, and Nancy was at the wheel. Her grandfather was eating the lunch they had brought so he wasn't really paying attention to where she was going. She was driving sideways on a slope when she suddenly realized the slope had become very steep.

"I became frightened, immediately put on the brakes, and asked my grandfather if he thought he should drive since I didn't think I could handle it," recalls Nancy. "He looked up from the cold fried chicken he was munching on, looked around at our situation, and said, 'Naw, you're doing fine.' He went back to eating the chicken, totally unconcerned."

Nancy says what her grandfather did that day taught her two lessons she has never forgotten:

1. He made it very clear that he trusted her to handle a difficult, even dangerous, situation. She respected her grandfather's judgement a great deal, and his belief in her helped Nancy to learn to believe in herself.
2. Nancy realized how limiting her own beliefs could be. When she didn't think she could handle the vehicle, she felt frightened and paralyzed. A moment later, when her grandfather convinced her she could handle it, her fear was gone and she was able to drive off the mountainside with ease. She learned that she was more capable than even she believed.

Says Nancy, "Since that day, my life has been an exploration to find out how much I'm actually capable of doing if I just believe I can. It never occurs to me that I can't do something unless I've actually tried it. The experiences have been fascinating and exhilarating. I'm convinced that most of our limitations are truly within our own minds."

Self-discovery and belief in oneself can happen in the most unexpected ways. Carmen and Nancy took different paths to arrive at a place where they believed in themselves, but they both got there. Understanding that "everything begins with you" is essential to acknowledging your abilities, respecting yourself, and doing what you love.

SOLO ADVENTURING

Sometimes a path you take to self-discovery is a literal path that you physically travel. Ten years ago, the idea of traveling alone had never appealed to me. Then I decided I wanted to go to Santa Fe, New Mexico, one year at Christmas, got in touch with a friend from high school who lived there, and stayed at his cabin in Tesuque, New Mexico, while he went home back east to be with his family.

At that time, I had never traveled alone, never ridden or driven across the country, or been on a Greyhound bus for longer than a few hours. Suddenly, I was on a 28-hour Greyhound bus ride, in the middle of winter, going across the United States, alone (not counting the 30 or so other passengers).

Upon my arrival in Santa Fe, I picked up a rental car and drove to the cabin. The drive was breathtaking and the cabin was set in a small, snowy valley surrounded by mountains. I soon discovered that the place had no running water, electricity, telephone, or heating system other than an old wood-burning stove. Quite a challenge for a young woman who had never even been camping and didn't know the meaning of "roughing it" except in a big city.

The next few days were spent in total solitude, trudging out in the snow to the lone toilet bowl positioned at the edge of a cliff, warming water on a kerosene stove to take sponge baths, and learning the fine art of making and maintaining a fire. I heard sounds I never had heard before, and more incredibly, heard silence. The six days at the cabin were filled with magical moments and self-discovery, learning that I could be alone and be quiet and everything would be OK.

More recently, I bought an old RV and have been driving around the country alone. This solo road trip has been an ongoing way to face the unknown and unfamiliar and trust that I will find my way.

Travelling alone can put you face to face with your fears of being alone. You begin to realize that being alone does not have to be the same thing as being lonely.

There is so much to do and to think about when alone—books to read, projects to finish, things to figure out, moments to accomplish something large or small. For me, being alone creates time to concentrate on my favorite thing—writing.

Here are two women whose individual travels led to learning and self-discovery and also influenced the way they do business.

The trip Kim Fisher took lasted three years. Today she is CEO of the technology company, AudioBasket, which allows customers to create personalized audio news and information broadcasts. But in 1994, having just finished business school, Kim moved to Lithuania. While there, she founded one of that country's first Web design businesses.

According to Kim, she learned the art of conversation while sitting at cafés for hours and talking with people from all over the world. She also learned how to:

- enjoy waiting in line and appreciate and take advantage of the worst situations.
- manage people who had no motivation to work.
- speak a new language, Lithuanian, and a part of another, Russian.
- really enjoy herself without a television or millions of other possible activities to choose from.

Something else Kim learned during her travels was flexibility, an invaluable skill in business. She learned to change her approach as a situation around her changed. One day, the economy would be developing and the next, the banking system would crash. While the business changes were extreme, she honed her ability to be adaptable and flexible.

She also learned patience. "You are lucky to accomplish one thing in your day in Lithuania and you learn to appreciate that."

And, of course, networking skills. "When you go to a new country without knowing anyone, you learn how to meet new people."

Kim believes she changed as a person during her trip. "I was a Type-A personality and most likely always will be. However, I did become more reflective through this experience. I also became bolder. I started a business in Lithuania which, by comparison, is a very easy thing to accomplish in America."

A 1983 business trip to Saudi Arabia left a lasting impression on Liz Cobb, Founder and Executive Vice President of Incentive Systems. She had just been promoted, and her first task was to train an affiliate partner and international client on using the company's database management system software. While she did have knowledge of the software, she had never before taught a class.

At the time, it was difficult for a woman to obtain a travel visa to Saudi Arabia, so Liz's employer had to prove that no man in the world was more qualified than she was to teach the class. They managed to get her a visa, and she was thrust into culture shock.

The experience was eye-opening for Liz. Outside her client's company "compound," a woman could be arrested if she was not properly attired. The Saudi women on the compound wore traditional clothing, completely covered from head to toe, including their faces, and viewed the world through thin black veils. Only their hands could be seen.

"I found the culture oppressive and confining," admits Liz. "As time passed, I found my female ego was being worn down." Although she was going through a difficult emotional adjustment to her environment, her classes ran successfully. However, when she taught sessions to a broader audience, she faced the Saudi culture's attitude toward women head-on, including being heckled by a Saudi male as she presented an overview of the company's software.

During her trip, Liz learned the importance of finding out what she didn't know. She would not have made it through the course if she hadn't thoroughly prepared for it in advance. She also wisely lined up a more senior person back in the States to answer her questions on a daily basis, despite the 16-hour time difference.

While teaching in a foreign country, Liz learned to focus on credibility, and saw that if you have information that is needed and valued by others, you can often overcome any prejudice you might face.

Ironically, the lessons Liz learned in Saudi Arabia were very relevant when she left her job and began to raise the first round of financing for her new business at a time when less than 5 percent of all venture money went to women. Says Liz, "Focusing on credibility meant that my business plan was more thorough than most. The facts were solid. And I actively solicited help from experts in finance, law, and accounting." Persistence and good manners, skills she had to have in Saudi Arabia to get anything done, also served her well as she dealt with the venture capital community.

Learning often comes in unexpected ways, from the most mundane to the most challenging or unusual experiences. Both Kim and Liz faced challenges as they conducted business in foreign countries, and learned new skills that worked well for them when they returned to the United States.

Being constantly open to the process of learning is essential to moving forward, both in your business and your personal life. As a business leader, if you sit back and "rest on your laurels," feeling confident you know all you need to, the world will quickly change around you and leave you behind.

Always remember the sense of wonder you had as a child. If you can retain that sense of wonder and a childlike curiosity about everything around you, you will continuously learn and grow. The ability to learn is often our antidote to unexpected change in our lives. It can be the powerful force that will open new doors, even after other doors have closed. Learning is the light we can shine on every situation to see our way down any path we choose.

PERSONAL PROJECT #1:
HONOR THE STUDENT WITHIN

If you haven't taken a class since the last time you were formally enrolled in school, take a class now. No more excuses about "not enough time." Some courses only meet once a month for a few hours. With a little research, you can find a course that satisfies your curiosity and fits your busy schedule.

Go the traditional route and contact your local universities for information on their continuing education programs or seek out a continuing education company like the Learning Annex. Look for a course that strikes your fancy.

Remember: You do not have to take a course directly related to your business. Taking creative writing or a class on medieval literature might sound random, but you will stimulate your mind in new ways. In business, fresh ideas and sharp thinking are two of your greatest assets.

You can also go online to take a class. See the end of this chapter for a list of online learning resources. Now you don't have to travel to a classroom to have formal instruction. Just click your mouse in the comfort of your home or office and learn something new.

PERSONAL PROJECT #2:

THE SOLO ADVENTURE FOR THE SOUL

Taking a trip on your own doesn't have to be an adrenaline-charged, physically-challenging adventure, although if you are game for one of those, get online or call your travel agent right now and book the trip.

Solo adventures can be as simple as checking into a bed and breakfast in the next town for the weekend to spend time alone reading a good book. Or spending a day in your hometown pretending you are a tourist and doing all of the sightseeing you always recommend to visiting friends and relatives but never do yourself. Or sitting in a local café, preferably on a nice sunny day at an outside table, to people-watch, write in your journal, or sketch someone sitting next to you.

Try taking a Greyhound bus or Amtrak train to a random destination chosen solely because it is a four-hour ride from your home. Start early in the morning, then upon your arrival, get out of the bus, get into a cab, and ask for a recommendation of a good restaurant in the center of town. Have a quiet lunch by yourself, then stroll around the streets and window shop. Return home the same evening and the only costs of your solo adventure will be transportation and food.

Solo adventures can sometimes be planned out and taken with someone else, but make sure you establish an understanding in advance that you will each take time to enjoy the journey alone now and then.

Sometimes taking a trip with someone else can unexpectedly turn into a solo adventure because you've parted ways, lost one another, or feel isolated from your travel partner and tune into your own experience. If this happens, don't panic. Take a deep breath, assess your situation, and come up with a solution. You'll be fine.

Taking a solo adventure can be scary at first. Being alone, even in a crowd, can quicken your pulse and cause you to sweat a little more than usual. But after the initial fear subsides, you'll feel exhilarated and recharged. Take your journey.

POWERTOOL 3 CHECKLIST

Learn Constantly

- *Yes, you can "teach an old dog new tricks" and all it takes is enrolling in a class, no matter how short in duration, to feel the energy of learning.*
- *Don't feel confined to taking classes solely related to your business. Experiment, explore, and discover.*
- *If you learn best by doing, get out there and do something new.*
- *Take the time to learn more about yourself. And don't forget to test yourself every chance you get.*
- *Take a trip alone. Your own personal adventure can teach you amazing things about yourself and the world around you.*

NUGGETS

MY FAVORITE BOOKS ON WOMEN'S SOLO TRAVELS

Another Wilderness: Notes from the New Outdoorswoman, Susan Fox Rogers, ed., Seal Press, 1997

Gifts of the Wild: A Woman's Book of Adventure, Faith Conlon, et.al., Seal Press, 1998

A Journey of One's Own: Uncommon Advice for the Independent Woman Traveler, Thalia Zapata, Eighth Mountain Press, 1996

Miles from Nowhere: A Round the World Bicycle Adventure, Barbara Savage, Mountaineers Books, 1985*

Solo: On Her Own Adventure, Susan Fox Rogers, ed., Seal Press, 1996
Tracks, Robyn Davidson, Vintage, 1980
Travelers' Tales: Gutsy Women, Travel Tips and Wisdom for the Road, Mary
    Beth Bond, Travelers' Tales, Inc., 1996
Traveler's Tales: Women in the Wild, Lucy McCauley, ed., Travelers' Tales,
    Inc., 1998
A Woman's Passion for Travel: More True Stories from a Woman's World, Mary
    Beth Bond and Pamela Michael, eds., Travelers' Tales, Inc., 1999
A Woman's World, Mary Beth Bond, ed., Travelers' Tales, Inc., 1995
Women Travel: First-hand Accounts from More Than 60 Countries, Natania
    Jansz, Miranda Davies, Emma Drew, and Lori McDougall, eds., The
    Rough Guides, 1999

* One of my personal favorites. Barbara Savage traveled with her husband,
    however, her writing delves into her own personal experiences and transfor-
    mations during the journey.

BUSINESS BOOKS I RECOMMEND

Some books I recommend that aren't necessarily typical business books
but really got me thinking about everything from leadership to power:

The Corporate Mystic: A Guidebook for Visionaries with Their Feet on the Ground,
    Gay Hendricks and Kate Ludeman, Dell Publishing Group, 1997
The Female Advantage, Sally Helgesen, Currency/Doubleday, 1995
In Our Wildest Dreams, Joline Godfrey, Harperbusiness, 1993
Princessa Machiavelli, Harriet Rubin, Dell, 1998

GENERAL COURSES ONLINE

Element K from Ziff Davis—www.elementk.com
Virtual University—www.vu.org
eCollege—www.ecollege.com
World Wide Learn—www.worldwidelearn.com

BUSINESS COURSES ONLINE

Jones International University—www.jonesinternational.edu
Goergia GLOBE (Global Learning Online for Business and Education)—
    www.georgia-globe.org
Keller Graduate School of Management—www.keller.edu
The Open University—www.open.ac.uk

Chapter 4

OVERCOME CRISIS

And Use It to Gain Wisdom

"The great crises of life are not, I think, necessarily those which are in themselves the hardest to bear, but those for which we are least prepared."

—Mary Adams, 1902

TODAY MARY SCHANZER IS OWNER OF PARTY PERSONNEL, LLC. BUT in 1991, at age 35, she was bankrupt. The restaurant she and her husband had opened ten months earlier had failed, and they were penniless. They lost their house, cars, and almost their marriage, but according to Mary, "we couldn't afford a divorce attorney."

Being broke was a catalyst for Mary. She was determined to do everything possible to recover financially and to keep her marriage intact. While working full time as a receptionist at a beauty salon, she took an additional job at a banquet facility managing off-site catering. There she saw a need for qualified wait staff and bartenders to work catered events and parties and in 1993, she started Party Personnel.

Mary's financial crisis and business failure made her reexamine her priorities. She realized her family came first. She changed her life to be the mom she wanted to be, then built a business that fit her life.

MY OWN CRISIS

For some women, the catalyst for making significant change is a crisis, some bad thing that happens to them or someone they love. Don't create crisis as the motivator for pursuing your true path, but if a crisis does occur, don't let it cause you to lose sight of where you want to be.

Several years before I finally pursued my writing full time—my lifelong dream—something happened that made me change the course of my life. In August of 1994, my friend and I were held up at gunpoint and kidnapped on the Upper West Side of Manhattan. One o'clock in the morning, three guys, three guns, and 15 minutes of fear while we were taken against our will from my friend's apartment to the bank and back out onto the street. We finally managed to escape.

That terrifying event changed the entire way I viewed my life, particularly the way work dominated what I did. I saw that working for others was not fulfilling my own dreams and ambitions. To regroup, I left New York City and my job at a nonprofit organization to visit my sister in Santa Fe, New Mexico, for a few months. While there, I decided not to work for anyone else again, and spent my time contemplating starting a business, making a list of skills, and searching for a suitable business idea.

What did I know how to do? I knew how to write, had marketing and public relations experience from previous jobs, and loved using the Internet as a hobby. While in Santa Fe, I took a one-hour course in HTML for $10, learning about the Web and how to build web sites. That led to starting a Web Development and Online Marketing company—Cybergrrl, Inc.—in 1995, before most people even knew that the Internet existed.

After having a 9mm gun pointed at me and living to tell the story, my whole view of life changed drastically. Some people might be completely overcome by such a harrowing experience, falling into a depression or living life in fear. I faced my fears head-on and embarked on a major professional challenge—starting a business—to make something positive out of something so negative. Starting a business was a symbolic gesture—not an end goal—that gave me more control over my creativity and destiny.

For some women, reexamining their lives only happens during a severe illness or near-death experience. Why do we wait until something bad happens before looking closely at how we are working or living our lives?

Do not wait for a crisis to learn how you should be living your life. But if one does occur, know that on the other end of every crisis is the opportunity for self-discovery, strength, and a new path.

Don't let a crisis get you down.

TURNING AROUND PROFESSIONAL CRISIS

When crisis strikes at work, it can shake your confidence and affect not only your professional life, but your personal life as well. You could choose to look at getting fired from a job as change that is happening to you. Or you can find the strength within to take charge of that change and create opportunity from the situation instead of being beaten by it.

Sometimes being fired can be a devastating experience that creates a genuine life crisis. How does one find the strength to go on? Here is one woman who took a painful journey beyond her professional setback to recreate her professional life.

Lorraine Aho, founder and CEO of SacredHome.com, discovered how difficult being fired can be when you are far from familiar surroundings. In late 1998, Lorraine had all the appearances of professional success. She received a promotion to a national sales management position for an up-and-coming software company that included a large salary increase and a move from San Francisco to Chicago.

On the first of January 1999, she was let go without cause or warning. Her husband hadn't even had time to find a job in their new location, so they were both unemployed and 2000 miles away from friends and family. She was in shock after being fired and developed health problems related to the stress, gaining 30 pounds. She and her husband lived out of their pickup truck with their two cats, traveling the country and camping out with relatives and in state parks for six months while they struggled to get back on their feet.

Lorraine kept a journal during that difficult time.

Journal Entry, April 1999

On the surface, our lives seem unfocused, uncertain, disjointed. But I believe that we were purposefully taken apart, down to the core, in order to be rebuilt and remade better than we were.

Lorraine felt emotionally shattered and couldn't imagine handling interviewing for a new job, rejection, or even giving 100 percent of herself to a job and being vulnerable to an employer. She felt there was no other alternative than working for herself.

Journal Entry, May 1999

Happy Birthday to me! Today I am 35. This is not what I imagined 35 would be like. It always seemed old and stodgy to me. But now that I am 35, it feels great! I looked into the mirror today and saw an artist, a free spirit, an adventuress. All of my horoscopes say that today is the first day of the rest of my life, and I'm feeling that way. Halftime is over. Put me in, Coach. I'm ready to kick some butt out there, and start winning. I spent the first half of the game on the sidelines, and now I understand the game and the rules and I'm ready to start participating in the game of life!

Lorraine took time to rest and meditate, using her energy to focus on herself. She began to pay attention to the "little things in life," finding joy in "tiny pleasures." She stopped rushing around and concentrated on slowing her life down to a more manageable pace.

After spending months researching e-commerce companies, talking with SBA and SCORE volunteers, reading books, and formulating a business plan, Lorraine started a web-based business selling spiritual arts and crafts. Lorraine and her husband began settling into a new place.

"Although I lost all of the external trappings of success—home, job, and 'stuff'—I gained the most important gifts a person could want—self-respect, joy, and optimism about the future," says Lorraine. "I lost everything and yet gained everything."

RISING UP FROM PERSONAL CRISIS

A crisis occurring close to home is too often the wake-up call to women who are living a life they think they should instead of the one they want. Whether the crisis is facing the illness or death of a loved one or dealing with their own serious illness or an accident that puts them near death, women often find their real strengths and true selves at the lowest points of their lives.

IF YOU DON'T HAVE YOUR HEALTH

When you are healthy, it is all too common to take it for granted. You work hard, living to work rather than working to live. You are a machine, superhuman, Wonder Woman, invincible. And then you get sick, sometimes suddenly and without warning, but more likely with numerous warnings that you brush aside as you remember something else you have to get done, most likely at the office.

Being stricken with a severe illness can not only be terrifying, it can also make you feel as if you've lost control, no matter how confident and prepared you usually feel. Dealing with illness and coming back to health becomes not only a physical struggle, but a mental and emotional one as well. Here is one woman who took that journey and learned some valuable lessons.

For Suzi Berman, starting and growing her design business, D Media, was a very deliberate and careful process. She left no margin for error or failure by managing a slow and steady growth over several years and then carefully planning for the birth of her first child and a six-week maternity leave.

Four weeks after her child's birth, the challenges suddenly took an unexpected turn when she collapsed at a supermarket with excruciating pain in her leg. During the next four months, the pain Suzi experienced got worse, spreading to her other leg and both arms. Under the supervision of five different doctors, she underwent a multitude of tests, including nerve tests, MRIs, a sonogram, blood tests, a spinal tap that caused her to be rushed to the hospital for a blood patch procedure and the most painful test, a bone marrow biopsy.

Throughout her health ordeal, Suzi continued to work, running her business after her maternity leave ended. During that time, however, she was unable to drive, could not walk unassisted, and was taking prescribed painkillers to get through the day. Being the only salesperson in her company and responsible for all client interaction, Suzi was suddenly unable to handle all of her usual tasks.

She was finally diagnosed with Gaucher's Disease, a rare genetic disorder that causes an enzyme deficiency affecting the bones, and began treatment with an infusion of a synthetic form of the enzyme. By the time her treatment started, she was already in a wheelchair.

How did her business survive? Without any active sales force and no new clients or projects, Suzi was forced to inform a newly-hired staff member to look for employment elsewhere. She tried to combat the failing sales brought on by her disability by cold-calling, sending sales letters, and asking clients, friends, and colleagues for help in referring prospects.

Suzi cites hard work, determination, creativity, and a positive outlook as the attributes that not only helped her start her business but kept it alive. She also points to her extremely supportive husband, staff members, family, friends, and associates who never let her down. As her health improved, so did her business.

Within six months, she was walking with a cane and driving again. She also landed three new accounts. A few months later, she didn't need the cane anymore, nor the special shoes she had been required to wear during the worst part of her illness. When her landlord went out of business and she lost her office space and was forced to move quickly, Suzi realized how easy that professional crisis seemed in comparison to what she had been through with her illness.

"My illness taught me that I am a survivor," says Suzi. She has gone on not just to survive, but to thrive.

Suzi faced a difficult illness that could have devastated her entire life. But she persevered, despite great physical pain. She was forced to reexamine and discover new ways of achieving her goals. Even her goals changed as her illness brought to light what was really important to her.

THE UNEXPECTED ACCIDENT

Today, Heidi Van Arnem is the founder and CEO of iCan.com. When Heidi was 16, she went to a friend's house to drop off some clothes, a seemingly innocent task that nearly ended her life.

When her friend wasn't home, she went into her friend's brother's room. She found him sitting on his bed with a gun in his lap. After a short conversation, he brought the gun up and shot her, then screamed "I didn't know the gun was loaded." In a split second, her life changed forever. She was paralyzed from her neck down.

Being a quadriplegic hasn't prevented Heidi from achieving personal and professional success. She has become a leading advocate for the disabled, forming iCan.com, her second company, several years ago. Her first company, which she sold, was a travel agency for people with disabilities. Heidi has also invented and patented a lifting device for people with mobility impairments called the Slinger.

After her accident, Heidi's entire life was affected, particularly her self-esteem. At the time, she was a high school junior looking into universities. Despite constant health problems, pain, fatigue, and an overwhelming sense of loss, Heidi persevered, finishing high school and then college. She had 24-hour care and had to bring nurses to classes and even to parties.

Heidi took one day at a time, finding it hard to visualize a future for herself. She felt she had no value in life. Once she graduated, even getting a job was like a mystery to her. She felt lost. What could she do? Somewhere deep inside, she felt it was inevitable that she contribute to the world somehow. She wanted to be part of society, and just needed to figure out where to begin. She thought that she would be involved in improving opportunities for people with severe disabilities. Her first step was to sit on the board of a nonprofit in college.

When Heidi first went on job interviews right out of college, she was sure the people who interviewed her felt the same way she did—that she didn't know what she could do. Heidi decided to go to law school, but after she got sick at the end of her second semester, her dad—an entrepreneur—suggested that she start her own business instead of returning to school.

She decided to start a travel business and within a few months, had a full-service accredited travel agency. She sold the agency once she saw her profit margin shrinking, but already knew she would begin building iCan months before she sold her company. She put together a business plan, raised some capital in an angel round and quickly began executing her plan.

Today Heidi tries to stay as independent as she can, and she hopes that the people who work with her say she "doesn't let her disability get in the way of what she needs to get done to run the business."

"It can be difficult and overwhelming trying to discover a career that gives you a feeling of accomplishment and pride," admits Heidi. "I recommend figuring out what makes you happy and what you do well. Then simply find a way to make money at it. Very few things in life come easy, and if at first you don't succeed, try until you do."

Additional advice that Heidi has for women moving past crisis is to stay focused, but don't be afraid to change your direction if needed. Surround yourself with people you respect, people who are smarter than you, and people you can trust to look out for you. Don't wait a single moment for that special day to come when you will suddenly feel better or more motivated because chances are that day may never come. And, Heidi adds, "Remember to have fun!"

Heidi experienced a frightening accident and came face to face with the shortness of life. Instead of crawling into a hole and hiding from some harsh realities, she pushed past fear and uncertainty and began discovering her own path.

HITTING TOO CLOSE TO HOME

When difficulty or tragedy hits close to home by affecting members of our own family, we tend to put our lives on hold to deal with the crisis. At 31, Michelle Lemmons-Poscente, now president of International Speakers Bureau, received a call from her mother that her father, who was suffering from chronic heart disease, had been given three weeks to live. Leaving behind Los Angeles and an independent film she was trying to get produced, she headed for West Texas to help care for her father.

While in Los Angeles, Michelle had taken a part-time, flexible sales and marketing job promoting two speakers and booking their engagements, a position she could still hold while in Texas. One of the speakers agreed to loan her $7,500, and she used the money to found International Speakers Bureau (ISB) from a spare bedroom in her father's house. While she was establishing her business, she even took a job picking pecans to make ends meet.

Michelle's father died in her arms ten months after she had arrived in Texas, an experience that grounded her. While living in LA, she had been caught up in a different set of values, but coming home she realized it doesn't matter if you drive a Mercedes or a BMW. If you died today, would you have any regrets? Michelle realized she could honestly say that, as a result of the decisions she made right before and after her father's death, she would have no regrets.

It wasn't until after her father's death that Michelle began to think of ISB as a full-time career rather than just a way of bringing in some money. She finally moved her company to an office in Dallas, then added people to her team, growing her business in phases.

Michelle admits that even before she learned about her father's failing health, she had reached a pivotal moment in her life. She had "put her life on hold," not caring what happened when she woke up in the morning, and that feeling scared her into deciding to reclaim her life. She walked away from nice cars, expensive jewelry, and a big house to live life on her own terms.

Today Michelle has a booming business, three children, and a husband whom she met through her business. "I find my balance week by week or even project by project. I've really been an entrepreneur for as long as I can remember, in part because I have more flexibility than a regular job. The flip side, however, is that you can't make your own business successful without hard work, which means long hours. So the key is really finding a way to make things work within your specific circumstances."

Julie Cook Downing also gave up her career—one in human resources—to become a full-time, long-distance caregiver to first her mother and then her father. Because of her own experiences, she started a business based around the needs of caregivers, Caregiver's Comfort™ Creations, LLC.

Julie developed the concepts for her company during her frequent trips to Cleveland to support her father who was, at the time, caring for her mother. "I thought about my dad's emotional caregiving needs and about the importance of my mother receiving the very best care in the world. I decided that a line of gift products expressing appreciation to the caregiver was what the world needed."

Her first product, a book called *Caregiver's Comfort*™, was an inspirational journal, resource, and record book for caregivers that she dedicated to her father. Today, Caregiver's Comfort™ Creations, LLC, produces motivational tools and provides resources and seminars for the growing population of caregivers. Julie is also an author and speaker on the subject of caregiving, turning her personal experiences into inspirational lessons.

Michelle and Julie would be the first to admit that what they went through was not easy. Each had to find the right way to restructure their professional lives to get through personal challenges. Yet each one of them was determined to follow through with their professional vision and find balance amidst the chaos of family crises. They also discovered that by putting their family first in times of crisis, they were able to live and work with their priorities in an order that felt right to them. Their businesses were still able to grow and thrive, and they can look back at the choices they made during difficult times without regret.

COPING WITH THE EMOTIONAL SPLIT

If your health is failing, it can be a rude awakening to your own mortality and physical limitations. The failure of a close relationship, such as a marriage that ends in divorce, can be equally jarring, both emotionally and physically. So many women tend to base their self-image on their relationships, creating a barrier to their own personal growth that is only evident once the relationship is gone.

Patsy Bruce, now president and CEO of PAB Corporation, faced many of the same emotions and challenges as those faced by many women getting a divorce, however, she had the additional burden of splitting up "everybody's favorite couple" in the public eye. Patsy jokes that for many years she thought her first name was "Ed and," just as she was sure her husband thought his middle name was "and Patsy," as in "Ed and Patsy Bruce."

As one-half of the successful songwriting team that cowrote many hit songs in the '70s and '80s, including the enormous hit "Mammas, Don't Let Your Babies Grow Up to Be Cowboys," Patsy and her husband seemed inseparable. Then Patsy realized her 25-year marriage and business partnership was coming to an end when she discovered her husband was having an affair.

Thinking of herself as a "freestanding person" took Patsy longer than it did anyone around her. With her identity so tied to her husband and marriage, (she also ran a talent agency that represented him as a singer and actor), she knew she had to start a business that did not involve him.

Once she finally realized that people expected to deal with her, not her husband, she was able to see herself as independent. She started a special events company, Events Unlimited, and within two years had signed Fortune 500 companies to produce events for their conventions.

Five years after starting her events company, Patsy needed a place for her clients to meet. She chose her house, and soon other people began to ask to meet there, too. She converted the house into a successful country inn, and running it became another business venture.

In the early '90s, Patsy started a television production company with a friend. The show, and her events company, needed sets and scenic props, so she started a set building company called Nashville Scenic.

Patsy attributes her entrepreneurial spirit and business successes to the encouragement she received from the grandparents who raised her. She says they always encouraged her, telling her she could do anything she wanted to.

Patsy also acknowledges her faith in God and her friends as major sources of strength during low points in her life. "I think God does these things to teach us endurance," says Patsy "and thus we come out the other side with strength and patience."

Patsy believes women can reinvent themselves out of a failed marriage or career. "It takes visualizing where you want to be and setting a goal of getting there and never letting up until you—yes, you personally—change that goal. Never let anyone but you change the plan. Take advice from others and see how to fit it into achieving your plan."

Today Patsy has returned to writing. She is seven chapters into writing a book and also writes freelance articles and restaurant reviews for various magazines. After taking a long hiatus from songwriting—something that had been painful after her divorce—she has finally started accepting appointments for songwriting collaboration.

LIKE A PHOENIX

We've heard from some incredibly resilient women who were able to find their greatest strengths during their darkest personal and professional moments. As I was gathering their stories, I kept thinking of a phoenix—the mythical creature that rose from the ashes—as a symbol of women's ability to create positive opportunity out of negative situations.

Here is one woman who had an experience that took the phoenix metaphor to the extreme.

Ten years ago, Cynthia Harris stood looking at a charred lot in the Oakland Hills that just that morning had been her home and place of business. Her company was only a year old when the Oakland Hills firestorm destroyed everything she had, including hundreds of client press kits she was planning to bring to a major industry trade show that day.

Cynthia decided to attend the trade show as planned, more as a knee-jerk reaction rather than something she thought through. A client was depending on her to be at the show with the press kits and run media relations for the day, and Cynthia felt she needed to honor her commitment. The hardest part for her was buying a new ticket to Las Vegas to replace the burned one and then getting on the plane completely empty-handed, with no press kits and no luggage at all.

The generosity of others started while she was on the plane to Las Vegas. The woman sitting next to her learned Cynthia had just lost everything in the fire, assessed that she and Cynthia were about the same size, and gave her a beautiful suit right out of her garment bag. Even her community played a supportive role in rebuilding her business and her life.

Cynthia's company, Strategy Associates, now employs three dozen people in its Silicon Valley headquarters and Seattle, Boston, and London offices, and is consistently listed among the top 20 agencies in both the Silicon Valley and San Francisco Bay area.

Looking back at the last ten years, Cynthia admits that, internally, she did struggle with what had happened to her. "I had to stop asking, 'Why did this happen?' and learn to trust my faith that '. . . in all things God works for the good of those who love Him' (Rom. 8:28). This meant letting go of the idea that I could control what happened, too. A rather simple biblical proverb also helped get me through a lot—'When a man falls down, does he not get up?' That was it in a nutshell, really. What choice did I have but to persevere? I drew a lot of strength from God and the support of all the people around me."

Perseverance, character, and hope seem to be three qualities exhibited by the women in this chapter and this book. These women will be the first to tell you that you should not wait for a crisis to happen before you do what you love. And each of them has proven that a crisis might feel like the end but can also be another beginning.

Because women tend to be so finely attuned to the way the personal and professional sides of their lives are inextricably interconnected, the transformations that take place in times of crisis affect every aspect of their lives, including their work.

If you are going through crisis, take care of and believe in yourself. Know that you are not alone. Once you get to the other side of the crisis, use what you have learned to build something positive.

PERSONAL PROJECT #1:
THE ESSENTIAL "YOU" DAY

During times of crisis, we forget ourselves, most likely because we have to detach from our emotions to make it through a trying time. Forgetting ourselves can be our survival mechanism.

But taking care of ourselves during difficult times, is the most essential strategy for getting through the challenges, highs and lows, and emotional strains. Pull out a calendar and spend 20 minutes thinking of what you can do for yourself every day for a month. Write them on a calendar and then check that calendar daily and take action. Make the activities easy to do on your own or with minimal participation from someone else.

Here are a few ideas for essential "You" moments each day. Some may sound corny, but sometimes the corniest ideas have the most positive emotional impact. Why? Because we tend to do away with corny, silly, trivial, and frivolous things as we "grow up," and if we haven't yet, they are certainly the first things to go when something bad happens.

- Be playful or mischievous. Buy yourself a huge bouquet of flowers or a bunch of helium balloons for your home or office. Indulge in a single piece of mouth-watering chocolate from an expensive chocolatier. Treat yourself!
- Write a poem. Make sure it rhymes. This will take a little time so enjoy the moments and let creativity.
- Take that bubble or herbal bath that every woman always talks about taking but never does. Go all out, with candles, soft music, a glass of wine. Dim the lights, shut the door, and soak. Then give yourself a facial, manicure, or pedicure. Revel in the relaxing and nurturing sense of touch.
- Breathe from your stomach. Place a book on your stomach. Do not let your chest rise and fall but instead, concentrate on making the book rise and fall. Yogis practice the art of breathing from their stomach and believe it increases oxygen flow to the brain and other parts of their body, creating a calming yet invigorating affect.

Don't forget to breathe.

PERSONAL PROJECT #2: JOURNALING FOR HEALING
WRITE DOWN WHAT YOU'RE THINKING, FEELING, EXPERIENCING

B uy a blank journal from your favorite book or stationery store, find a great pen, and start writing. Make sure the journal is small enough to carry with you on business trips, to meetings, and to and from work so it is always handy when you have a thought you'd like to record.

Plagued with journal writer's block? Don't put pressure on yourself to write something incredibly insightful or poetic. Think of this journal as a book of stories—stories you have heard that you want to remember and stories about your own experiences that you'd want to tell someone if they came to you for advice. Or think of it as an outlet for your thoughts and feelings.

If writing isn't your thing, you can use the journal to store inspiring clippings from magazines and newspapers or copy down poems or quotes you've read or heard that strike a chord. You may also want to jot down comments or notes about the articles or poems, saying what they made you think of or what you did after reading them. Review your journal over time and revel in the wisdom you have gained.

Writing down thoughts has been a means of healing for so many people. Once you give yourself the freedom to write and honor your words, thoughts, and feelings, you'll feel a great sense of relief. You will also have an important document about your personal growth, particularly through a time of crisis.

And a final word of advice—buy a diary with a lock on it or keep your journal in a locked box when you don't have it with you. Sometimes, the greatest obstacle to writing down one's words is the fear of having them discovered by someone else without your consent. This journal is for you and you alone.

POWERTOOL 4 CHECKLIST
Don't Wait for a Crisis

- *Crisis at work is not the end of your world. Always remember you are greater than your job or business.*
- *Personal crises are tests and if you have faith—in whatever form that takes—you will pass the tests.*
- *A strong support network is key for any smart woman and can be indispensable during crisis. Be good to your supporters.*
- *In times of crisis, never forget to take care of yourself first.*

NUGGETS

BOOKS ABOUT CREATIVE WRITING AND JOURNALING

Journaling from the Heart, Eldonna Bouton, Whole Heart Publications, 2000

The New Diary: How to Use a Journal for Self-Guidance and Expanded Creativity, Tristine Rainer, JP Tarcher, 1979

Visual Journaling: Going Deeper Than Words, Barbara Ganim, Susan Fox, Quest Books, 1999

Wild Mind: Living the Writer's Life, Natalie Goldberg, Bantam, 1990

Writing Down the Bones: Freeing the Writer Within, Natalie Goldberg, Shambhala, 1986

A Year in the Life: Journaling for Self Discovery, Sheila Bender, Writers Digest Books, 2000

FEMALE MOTIVATIONAL SPEAKERS

Chances are, you have heard of motivational speakers such as Anthony Robbins, Zig Ziglar, and Stephen Covey. But can you name any female motivational speakers? Well, they are out there, and here's a short list of women who speak about women-specific issues or about general business or life issues from a woman's perspective. These audio tapes are perfect listening material while you are stuck in traffic or working out with your Walkman.

Julie White
> *Professional Impact/Personal Power*
> *Self-Esteem for Women*

Rita Davenport
> *It's Time for You*

Laura Berman Fortgang
> *Take Yourself to the Top*

Cheryl Richardson
> *Take Time for Your Life*
> *Life Makeovers*

Chapter 5

TACKLE TECHNOLOGY

Make It Your Tool to Help Accomplish Your Goals

"If we each help one other woman get online, we'll create a legacy of technical savvy and connectedness…for our daughters and granddaughters."

—Aliza Sherman

WHEN KATHY LONG'S HUSBAND TOLD HER SHE NEEDED TO GET A job because of the recession, Kathy, who is now head of Kat and Mouse Web Design, panicked. Her only job experience was at the local Dairy Queen 18 years earlier, and she had dropped out of college while pregnant with her first child to become a full-time mom.

With encouragement from a friend, Kathy enrolled in a local community college to learn WordPerfect. After one semester, she landed a temp job at a local high-tech company where she taught herself how to use a computer mouse, Windows operating system, and various software programs. Three months later, Kathy bought her own computer to practice her newly learned skills at home.

After reading books and taking numerous courses, Kathy entered the graphic design field. Then, following additional studies, she transformed her traditional graphic skills into Web skills and started her own Web design business. By taking charge of technology, she created the ideal business for herself.

TOUCHING TECHNOLOGY

In school, nobody could have ever predicted that I would some-day own a technology company. Regardless of my ability in math and science in grade school, I was encouraged to become an English teacher.

And computers? I never touched a computer until after gradua-tion, when I learned to use one while temping as a secretary. My boss suggested I could make a few dollars more an hour with computer skills. Who knew that those typing skills from ninth grade would come in handy!

My first computer was an Amstrad 1640, dual floppy—no hard drive—and a dot matrix printer. Its sole purpose was to output neatly formatted manuscripts to fulfill my dreams of becoming a published writer.

The friend who helped me purchase a computer also taught me how to "go online." Back then, "going online" meant connecting to local BBS's (Bulletin Board Systems) which were often nothing more than computers in someone's basement or bedroom. In those early years, everyone who connected to those systems spent a lot of time playing online games.

One night, on the computer as usual, I was startled when a mes-sage flashed across the computer screen. "Do you want to chat?" I jumped out of my chair, heart pounding, and ran to the windows to shut the blinds. Someone was watching me. Or worse yet: my com-puter had come alive and was talking to me. Finally, I returned to my desk and calmly typed "Hello." A response came back from a 17-year-old boy in Brooklyn.

In that instant, the entire world opened up to me like one great big door, and the computer was my key.

TURNING THE INTERNET INTO MY TOOL

After realizing that going online had potential beyond playing games, I left small BBS's behind and connected directly to the Internet.

The Internet was an astounding research tool for everything from health issues to ideas for my stories. As early as 1993, I was building and moderating forums online covering topics such as domestic violence and breast cancer. In 1994, discovering the World Wide Web while living in Santa Fe led to building my first web site—"The Web According to Cybergrrl"—and starting an Internet company out of my home. Suddenly, I was "Cybergrrl," champion of women online.

By looking at technology as a tool for doing something more efficiently—typing a manuscript, doing research, communicating with friends and family—I realized that there was nothing to be afraid of and there was everything to gain.

FROM "NO SKILLS" TO TECH BIZ

Even today, many women seem to have a similar story about how they went from no technology skills to starting a tech-oriented business. By taking classes, reading books, and spending hours developing new skills, they leverage technology to help build their businesses. Technology enables them to gain exciting new business opportunities, run their businesses more efficiently, market their businesses on a global scale, and gain the flexibility that online communication facilitates.

Today, Heidi Allen is founder and president of Knowledge Hound, LLC, but while pursuing her music career, Heidi got a long-awaited record deal. She signed the contract on the dotted line and gave away most of her possessions in order to move and start recording her first record. Then, without warning, the record label that signed her went out of business. She was suddenly in debt with nothing left to sell.

Using a friend's computer with Internet access, Heidi began to teach herself Web development skills. While she tried to find resources on the Web to help her learn, she realized how difficult it was to locate them. So she began to build a directory of how-to sites which turned into a business opportunity. Now, as a Web developer with a proven track record, she'll always be able to find good work and her future seems more secure. In an ironic twist, the security she gets from being a Web developer allows her to approach her music with less anxiety and more confidence.

Her advice to women who are shying away from technology? "The Internet is the easiest, most powerful way to help you achieve your dreams. You can find support, advice, tutorials, and opportunities for virtually anything you can imagine. You can meet knowledgeable people from around the world willing to share hard-to-come-by information. You can even make lifelong friends. All you have to do is decide on a goal and learn how to use the basic tools available. Dedicate some time and patience now, and your payoff will begin almost immediately."

Another musican, Brenda Kahn, president of WOMANROCK, went from being a "non-techie" to creating a web site geared toward other female musicians. Her Web business started, like Heidi's, through a glitch in her music career.

When her record label, Columbia Records, dropped her second album in 1995, she had no money, no real knowledge of computers, and no idea how she was going to run her music career without a label. Brenda knew that a computer could help her run her professional life. She could connect with fans through e-mail, write press releases, manage a budget and tour schedules, and create flyers, so she bought her first computer and taught herself Word (for word processing) and Excel (for spreadsheets).

Brenda soon discovered that the more she learned about computers and the Internet, the more she wanted to learn. To make ends meet, she took a part-time job at a company that did filings for the SEC online and taught herself additional computer software programs. Then her boyfriend taught her how to use Adobe PhotoShop, a graphics program, and she began designing her own artwork. Meanwhile, the music industry was turned upside down by the Internet, and Brenda recognized how independent recording artists could benefit from the ability to distribute and promote their music online.

She approached a fan who had been helping her maintain her own music web site with a business proposition. They would go into business together and start an online 'zine focused on women musicians. They launched WOMANROCK.com in 1999 with Brenda handling the editorial side and her music fan handling the Web development. Today, Brenda spends a lot of time going to conferences and seminars, and reading about new technology, always looking for ways it can help her in her work.

Brenda's advice is to be patient with yourself. "Men and women learn very differently and therefore teach very differently. Find someone you can connect with to be your coach or mentor." Although Brenda opted not to become a programmer herself, she teamed up with a programmer and developed a business concept that leveraged not only technology but her creative strengths and interests as well.

When Janet R. Young, a teacher, first went online, it wasn't for business. She had suddenly developed asthma and was mostly homebound for several months. Her son insisted that getting on the Internet would give her something to do.

Months later, when she asked her son what else she could do

on-line, he suggested that she build her own web site and bought her two books on HTML. Then the teacher in Janet took over and she decided to create a web site that her colleagues, students, and students' parents could use.

Janet developed Mrs. Young's Super Charged Educational Voyage (www.fortunecity.com/millenium/garston/49/), which evolved into an Internet-based newsletter, The Education Companion (www.fortunecity.com/millenium/garston/49/team2.html) and moderated a related discussion list (www.yahoogroups.com/group/the-education-companion/info.html).

She went on to create web sites for other people and soon decided to formally incorporate as a business. Says Janet, now president of her own technology company, JRY Development Corporation, "I am not a true techie, I hire contractors for that work. However, I have taught myself enough to build a company that effectively uses technology to deliver what it proposes, on time, and on budget."

E-QUOTE: MICHELLE LAWLOR,

FOUNDER AND CEO, EKINDNESS.COM

"I think if I could teach one woman anything else, it would be that we are all afraid of things we haven't done before. Feel afraid, talk about it if you have to, and then figure out how to get it done anyway. Take the time to learn [to use technology and the Internet]. There are many ways to use technology to gain back some time for yourself. Push yourself and try something new that is going to pay off tenfold for yourself."

STARTING A "DOTCOM"

You may not want to start an Internet company, but you can get some ideas or inspiration from the next several women whose companies exist because of the Internet.

For GirlGeeks CEO and cofounder Kristine Hanna, her first exposure to technology happened while working in television at Lorimar Studios in Los Angeles which, at the time, produced shows such as *Dallas* and *Max Headroom*. Video editing was fairly new and Kristine was fascinated by the technology and its creative possibilities.

In the late '90s, Kristine began to move away from television and film and focused her attention on the Internet and computer technology. She sought funding for a documentary film about successful women in technology as an inspirational learning tool to encourage other women and girls to get involved in technical fields.

As part of the documentary promotion she had planned an interactive web site to go along with the film. The web site quickly became the focus of her new company, GirlGeeks, and turned into an online community and commerce site offering career, training, and mentoring services for aspiring women in technology.

Kristine realized the power of the Internet to create an entirely new business and established a forum for others to gain technology skills and access tech resources. Says Kristine, "Technology is great for women looking to advance their careers. For the most part, it is an equal-opportunity field: if you are proficient, you will advance. Companies want and need qualified IT workers, both men and women."

While working at the largest antiquarian bookshop in the country in the early 1990s, Helen Driscoll, founder and director of Fine Paper Company and InviteSite.com, began using the Internet. Helen jokes that back then, at the rare bookshop, she was actually a human search engine, locating books and information for customers.

In late 1995, she left the bookshop, cashed in her pension plan, and used $15,000 of it to start her own company—Fine Paper Co.—and immediately setting up an Earthlink Internet account. "I do remember how weird it felt to use the Web," says Helen. "I thought I was going to break something or do something wrong. Or get lost." But she didn't, and soon Helen was using the Internet to correspond with other people around the world for advice and resources to build her business.

Her company's first web site went up in 1997, and over time, she envisioned a web site where customers could create designs right on the site. Before she approached programmers about her idea, she did her research, read developer and programmer magazines, and lurked in chat rooms and on message boards for Mac developers. By gaining an understanding of the concepts behind the technology, she was able to fully conceptualize the site she wanted to have built.

Self-funded and self-sufficient, Helen's second site, InviteSite.com, was born. The new site allowed customers to create invitations that they could print themselves on handmade or fine papers or that the Fine Paper Co. could letterpress for them.

Says Helen, "I find the concepts behind computers completely exciting and using them somewhat frustrating. You have to remember that using software is about learning the rules. But the root of 'technology' is Greek and means 'the method or technique of how we make art or the craft of art.' So technology is the use of tools to make art. That should chip away at some resistance to technology!"

Regardless of your background, whether you are a musician like Heidi or Brenda, a teacher like Janet, a filmmaker like Kristine, or a librarian like Helen, you may have an idea for a business based on your own expertise. By taking advantage of technology and the Internet, you can turn that business idea into reality.

THE INTERNET AS "ESSENTIAL BUSINESS TOOL"

Not all women who are familiar with the Internet go on to start technology-based companies. Instead, they incorporate the Internet into their non-technical businesses and gain a wide range of benefits from doing so.

Randy Epstein, president of My Red Shoes, LLC, learned how to use the Internet while interviewing for a job. Prior to going to an interview, she went online to get valuable background information and insights into companies where she was applying for work. Her ability to use the Internet proved useful to her back then and even more so when she decided to start her own business.

Today, Randy uses the Web in many ways for business, including:

- All correspondence with clients is via e-mail. She also sends out mass e-mailings to clients to update them on industry changes and new investor dollars that are available and to inform them about her upcoming presentations.
- All bills are paid on the Web, saving her business hundreds of dollars and countless hours each year in bookkeeping costs. Some web sites that can help with your bill-paying and business finances include PayMyBills.com and Quicken.com.
- All her research about companies and even the news she reads is retrieved from the Web. In the past year, the Web has saved her several thousands of dollars in legal and accounting fees as well as hundreds of dollars worth of subscriptions to industry trades.

Says Randy, "Over the long-term, using the Web will save you time and money, and help you establish creditability for your business."

One of the main reasons Phyllis del Pico, founder and director of RecruitersOnCall.com, first went online was to explore ways she could stay connected to family and friends. She became an early Web user when she listed her consulting business in an online directory. Potential clients were able to locate and connect to her either through telephone or e-mail and she was able to work at home while her children were young.

Working at home, alone, was also the catalyst for Phyllis's knack for tinkering with hardware and software. Since there was never anyone else around to help her fix something when it went wrong, she was forced to fix everything she could herself. She overcame her fear of technology the first time she opened up the computer and looked inside.

The Internet has saved Phyllis hours of time by reducing her efforts in locating the companies or candidates crucial to her recruiting business. With technology, she can run her business with a small staff and easily outsource extra work.

"You owe it to yourself to utilize every tool out there to help you with your business," advises Phyllis. "Take a class. Meet other women who are already [using the Internet] and learn from them. Don't waste another day wishing you knew something that is incredibly easy to learn."

As she approaches her 50th birthday, Phyllis emphasizes that it is never too late to learn.

> ### E-QUOTE: LORRAINE M. PASQUALI,
> ### FOUNDER AND PRESIDENT OF IMAGINESTATION
>
> *"Take a deep breath and dive in. Check your local community college for credit and noncredit classes, look for online resources, read books, attend seminars. As far as the business end of things, check your local Small Business Development Center, contact the SBA, take classes, and plan, plan, plan. Learning the technology is one thing; running a business is another."*

"I was 35 when I first went online," says Paula Quenemoen, one half of the twin-sister team that runs and owns Jagged Edge Mountain Gear. At first, she admits, she was clueless about the Internet, so she signed up for a $300 class at a local university. After her first lesson, she was hooked.

When her company installed a computer network, however, she found that her classes weren't enough to deal with tasks such as using the office e-mail system. "I burst into tears because I didn't know that I was suppose to retrieve the e-mail. I thought it just wasn't working, I didn't understand what I had to do, and was so frustrated." Since then, however, Paula is proud to say she has had no more technical problems, at least nothing that tech support hasn't been able to help her solve.

Paula's company, Jagged Edge, first debuted its web site—built by a high school student—in 1995. Looking back, Paula realizes how naïve she and her sister were about the Internet for business. They didn't realize that their young designer had used someone else's photograph without permission. That created a bit of a business crisis but luckily it was quickly resolved. Eventually, Paula and her sister turned to major technology companies like IBM to redo their entire office computer systems, upgrade their web site, and teach them important Internet business concepts.

Using Internet technology has given Paula and her staff flexibility in how and when they work. Says Paula, "I work more from my wonderful home. Working 12-hour days is common, but I can choose my hours. I may work until three in the morning and then go [rock] climbing in the daytime. When I don't have to deal with the commotion of the office and the affairs of the day-to-day, I'm much more effective and productive."

Saving time and money, establishing credibility, outsourcing work, working from home—as you can see from stories of women like Randy, Phyllis, and Paula, the Internet and technology can be your tool to accomplish a myriad of tasks and gain countless benefits.

There is no excuse good enough for failing to gain the knowledge and skills you need to constantly improve and grow as a person and as a businesswoman. Whether you use technology for communication or creativity, business or productivity, computers and the Internet should be your tools. Don't get left behind by refusing to learn about and use computers or the Internet. (OK, I'm stepping down from my soapbox now.)

PERSONAL PROJECT #1:
BUILD A WEB SITE OF YOUR OWN

Every woman should have a web site. You don't have a web site? Or you have a business web site but not a personal one? You can teach yourself HTML—Hypertext Markup Language or the basic building blocks of Web development—in just a few hours by using online resources. And believe it or not, the most difficult thing about HTML is the typing—it is that easy!

What could your web site be about? You can publish your poetry, or make a page for your family photos, or keep an online diary of your travels. You can link to web sites that you like or ones pertaining to your area of expertise. Your personal web site should be a place where you can express yourself. Just keep in mind that anyone in the world can access it.

If you aren't looking to learn HTML from scratch but want to experiment with something simple, there are web sites that let you set up your own site for free using and easy point-and-click interface.

Enjoy the process of experimenting with a web site of your own. Use it as a creative outlet. Building a web site is an "instant gratification" activity because you immediately see the results of your programming and any changes you make.

A little knowledge of HTML goes a long way and knowing the basics of building your own site can give you a better understanding of what is happening with your business web site when it is being built or redesigned. Becoming more familiar and comfortable with Web lingo and concepts can even help you navigate those painful but important conversations with your designer.

You can find a list of helpful books and web sites at the end of this chapter. Teach yourself a little HTML, put up your own site, and join the Web Revolution!

PERSONAL PROJECT #2:

TEACH SOMEONE HOW TO GO ONLINE

If you're using the Internet at work and at home and have discovered the many practical uses for e-mail and the Web, why not share this knowledge with another woman who isn't yet online?

There are many ways to find women who are still not online but who can benefit from the technology. When you network at women's professional business events, keep your ears open for women who confess they aren't yet online or glance at the business cards you collect and notice if any of them are missing e-mail or web site addresses. Offering to help a woman to get online can create a larger networking opportunity.

Another place to find women with whom you can share your computer and Internet skills is through a local nonprofit organization that works with women in need. Imagine the value of your sharing your knowledge with women at a battered woman's shelter or welfare-to-work program.

If you do offer to teach someone how to go online, set the parameters of the lessons and create a comfortable, non-threatening environment. Listen to the other person. What are their interests? What do they want to learn? How can the Internet benefit them or their business? Keep in mind that what interests you may not interest them.

Be patient. Once you have mastered the Internet, you may not recall how confusing and overwhelming it was when you first sat down and logged on. Get back in touch with that feeling and use it to have patience as you teach.

Sharing your knowledge of the Internet is an important way to make sure women don't get left behind as the way we all communicate and do business continues to be transformed by technology.

POWERTOOL 5 CHECKLIST

Use Technology as Your Tool

- *You do not have to be a "techie" to use technology as your tool, just a smart businesswoman.*
- *Don't be afraid to ask questions. Learn how to use technology from those who take the time to make sure you understand.*
- *Examine your business and recognize ways technology can improve operations.*
- *If you don't already have one, build a web site of your own. This should be in addition to your business site. Every woman should have her own web site.*
- *If you know how to use technology, share that knowledge with another woman or girl.*

NUGGETS

BOOKS TO TEACH YOURSELF BASIC WEB BUILDING

Creating Killer Web Sites, Second Edition, David Siegel, Hayden Books, 1997

HTML for Dummies, Ed Tittle et al, IDG Books Worldwide Inc, 1997

HTML: The Definitive Guide, Chuck Musciano, O'Reilly Books, 2000

Teach Yourself Web Publishing With HTML in 14 Days, Laura LeMay, Sams, 1999

WEB SITES WITH HTML TUTORIALS

HTML: An Interactive Tutorial for Beginners
    www.davesite.com/webstation/html

Writing HTML
    www.mcli.dist.maricopa.edu/tut/

WebMonkey: Authoring HTML Basics
     www.webmonkey.com/teachingtool/
HTML Primer
     www.htmlprimer.com

FREE WEB SITES

AOL Hometown
     hometown.aol.com
Geocities
     www.geocities.yahoo.com
Homestead
     www.homestead.com
Tripod
     www.tripod.lycos.com/build/sitebuilder/

Chapter 6

MOLD YOUR MISSION

Write Down Your Life's Purpose and Make It Real

"Nothing contributes so much to tranquilize the mind as a steady purpose—a point on which the soul may fix its intellectual eye."

—Mary Shelley

ANDREA KAY IS AN AUTHOR, SYNDICATED COLUMNIST, AND CAREER consultant for her company, Art of Self Direction. It was her personal mission that led her to start her dream business. As she was trying to figure out her career path, she discovered that many people were unhappy or confused about their careers. She made it her personal and professional mission to apply her strengths as a writer and public speaker to help others find their true path.

Today, Andrea focuses on helping others "discover their potential and create a plan to get there." She works with people "who feel unappreciated, misunderstood, overworked, underpaid, or unhappily employed, or who are unemployed to . . . discover what they can do and how to get it."

She continues to produce the weekly newspaper column she has written for the last 12 years. She has also published three books, had several radio shows and weekly television segments, and is now making her move to national radio and TV. She's a woman with a mission!

MY LIFELONG DREAM

A few years ago, while rummaging through old boxes at my mom's house, I found a piece of paper that was part of a writing assignment from the seventh grade. In response to the question, "What do you want to be when you grow up?" I had written:

"I want to be a writer so I can touch people's lives."

Throughout school, writing had been my hobby. After college came jobs as a waitress and a secretary at a temp agency. Next were careers in the music business, a stint as executive director at a nonprofit organization, and then head of an Internet company for five years.

During this entire time, I dreamed of being a published writer but never took the steps necessary to make the dream a reality. Then I found that piece of paper in a box. Seeing my lifelong dream in writing was very powerful and made it more real and tangible for me.

How had I managed to avoid my dream for so long? Why was I making career choices that deviated from my deepest goal? Luckily, I broke the pattern by turning my dream into a mission. Here's how I did it.

FROM DREAM TO MISSION

After five years running my business, I landed a second book deal. The first deal had come about by "accident" after *The Wall Street Journal* did a story on my Internet company, and I was approached by several publishers to write a book for women about the Internet. That book was written literally over the course of three weekends because there was a company to run, and there was no time to write.

Around the time I got a second book deal, I had found the piece of paper with my mission: to become a writer to touch people's lives.

With much trepidation, I decided to take a little time away from Cybergrrl, Inc., to write a second book and give my dream some room to breathe. Immediately, I knew that I was living my dream, even if only on a temporary basis, and it was exciting.

Toward the end of 1999, I made the difficult decision to sell Cybergrrl, Inc., to my business partner so that I could write full time. I was a woman with a mission, sending queries out to magazines and web sites for potential writing assignments.

After months without any response to those queries, I finally got a positive reply and one article led to another and then another. By September 2000, 70 percent of my income came from writing. I was a full-time writer!

As you can see, initially I had no direct path to becoming a full-time writer because I had no laser focus on that goal. I was just dreaming, not molding a mission, that singular purpose. A seventh-grade writing assignment had revealed my mission: touch people's lives through writing. Until writing took on the legitimacy and importance of a mission in my adult mind, it was not going to happen, at least not on a full-time basis.

A mission is a beacon to guide you to your true goals.

Here are several women who feel that putting their mission down on paper—in some tangible form—is an effective way to make that mission more attainable. They also give tips for molding your mission.

LIVING AND WORKING BY A MISSION

Carey Earle, president of the Harvest Consulting Group, wrote down the beginnings of a personal mission, or as she puts it, her "vision statement," in her first journal at eight years old. Her goal was, "to be the best girl I can be," and Carey says she still strives for that in her life today.

Carey is a big believer in taking the time to write things down. For her, seeing it on paper is always powerful, and gives her a place from which to evolve. She writes down her own mission and goals every year on January 1st or 2nd. She usually spends two to three hours reviewing old goals and seeing where she has come from and contemplating where she wants to go. She even buys fancy paper that feels good to the touch to give her hand the sense that what is written down is important.

After writing her mission on nice paper, Carey puts it into a neon green folder and positions it so it's the first thing she sees when she opens her personal filing cabinet at home. Even if she doesn't read through the folder constantly, the neon green color gives her a visual jolt, getting her synapses firing. Carey does read her personal mission statement every two months or so, especially when she is feeling frustrated, in order to get back on track.

Carey's personal and professional missions are tied closely together. Her business mission grew directly out of her and her business partner's personal goals and aspirations.

Harvest's Mission:

> *To inspire our clients, colleagues, and partners with innovative ideas, solutions, and service that build their businesses online and off.*

Carey Earle's Personal Mission:

- *To always act with integrity and grow personally and professionally by doing the best work.*

- *To succeed by my own strength and ideas—never compromise my values or beliefs for advancement.*
- *To always have the respect of my peers, employees, clients, and family.*
- *To take time to help people who are looking for jobs or are in career transition.*

Carey's personal mission has evolved over time. For example, five years ago she was working for a large advertising agency and her personal mission was to nurture her creativity outside of work because she felt stifled by the politics and hierarchy at her job. Conflicts with a co-worker began to eat away at her, and she reacted physically to what she was going through emotionally. She took a trip to Ireland and looked closely at what she was doing at work. Away from the pressure of her job, she realized that she was ignoring her personal mission. She wasn't being true to herself.

Carey returned from her trip and quit her job. She'll never forget the moment she took a ferry along the Hudson River, went to the deck, and screamed at the top of her lungs like Melanie Griffith's character in the movie *Working Girl*. "I felt like I'd gotten myself back and that I'd been holding my breath for a very long time. When you're living your mission, you are breathing. It's amazing how long we can go without breathing, but there is a high price you pay for that."

When Carey started her own business, creativity was no longer a problem. Therefore, her personal mission changed from focusing on creativity to being true to herself and bringing her personal core values to what she was doing every day. "When you're working on your own, you have the opportunity to bring who you are to life every day—no longer feeling the pressure to fit into someone else's idea of success."

THE CARE AND FEEDING OF YOUR MISSION

Itec Resources principal and managing director, Geetha P. Rajan's mission is to build solid, lasting relationships with people in her community. Even a line on her company web site echoes her mission: "At the end of the day, it's the relationships that define our business."

According to Geetha, realizing your mission is a process. It is defined and redefined by the passing of time and the realization of your dreams. Her professional mission has been defined by her professional experiences over the years. By listening to her clients and understanding what is important to them, she can deliver relevant services. Through communication and interaction, she builds that all-important relationship with her clients.

Geetha believes that most women know inside what they want to accomplish but too often look back and regret not doing something they wanted to do. "The key to realizing your mission is to know what your mission is. Define it. Write it out. Scribble it on a Post-it™ note and stick it on your computer. Use it as your screen saver. Work towards it every day and in every way possible. Consciousness is the key to realization. Staying focused and remaining positive is critical."

Joy Radle's main advice for establishing a mission and reaching your goals is to break each goal into manageable steps. "Once you have searched your soul to discover what it is, defined it, shaped it, dreamt, colored, and clarified it, then write it down in clear, achievable steps. Find out what it is you need to do to get there."

Joy believes that as you master intermediate steps on your way to achieving your goals, you will feel a sense of accomplishment and confidence to push forward. She also sees the whole process of finding your personal mission and living it as the means of discovering how to be true to yourself. For her, being true to herself meant "operating at the full capacity" of her talents in business. She realized the only way to accomplish her goals was to run her business on her own terms and gain financial independence.

Over time, Joy's mission began to change. Says Joy, "Once I had achieved success, sustained it, relocated the business to my desired

---

SHE READS

Recommended by Joy Radle, President and Founder, All MarCom, LLC

What Color Is Your Parachute? by Richard Nelson Bolles "[This is] an excellent manual to facilitate changing careers. If you're feeling stuck and uninspired by your current work, pick up this book. It helps you to itemize and validate your skills, and then inspires you to find new ways to apply them—based upon the premise that we enjoy doing what we do well in work and play."

Crossing the Chasm by Geoffrey A. Moore and Regis McKenna "[This is an] important manual for my field of work, the high-tech marketing industry. It discusses how important it is to segment and target specific audiences while taking a technological product to the mainstream market. It suggests a stepped roll-out strategy as well as a 'whole-product' development or packaging strategy to help consumers integrate technology into their daily lives."

Hitting the Sweet Spot
"This book coaches marketers to direct our attentions to the customer, rather than on our products' features. The sweet spot can be hit when we have the right amount of consumer insight and brand insight in combination. A practical how-to."

geographic location, and then lifted it above the million-dollar bar, my heart's desire shifted toward family. My goal of financial independence now includes a husband and two children. I've raised the bar in order to achieve my goal, and I'm staying true to my heart by striving toward it."

Orit, president and CEO of The O Group, built her company from a one-person design shop 15 years ago into a full-service marketing communications firm. She says that throughout the entire process, she has always adhered to her mission, which is expressed in her personal and professional mission statement:

Live and work with a passion about what you're doing—always doing the best work you can, being the most creative you can be and always enjoying and learning from the process.

Arriving at her all-encompassing mission happened at a young age. When she was a teenager, Orit didn't feel she belonged. In her mind, the other girls at school were always prettier and smarter, and they seemed to know what they wanted. Orit felt at odds with who and what she would become because she didn't want what anyone else wanted.

One day at school, she convinced her art teacher to let her focus on a project that she could not get out of her head, and it was then that she believes she "found herself" and her passion, although she did not fully realize it at the time.

Formalizing her mission statement wasn't a natural process for Orit. "Until you hear, read, and listen to other people talking about missions, I don't really think you think much about what a mission is. The formal process came [as I was] asked by different people what my mission was. I was then able to easily verbalize it, knowing it was something that had been a part of me forever."

Says Orit, "Don't be intimidated if you can't define your [mission] just yet. Give yourself time to grow and learn, and it will come."

Sometimes, you discover your mission when you least expect it. Janice Caillet, chief catalyst of Coaching Circles, a service of Partners In Life, Inc., discovered hers while jogging.

"I was running in Central Park a few years back when 'Bridge Over Troubled Water' came on over my walkman," says Janice. "Everything in the world clicked. I broke down in tears. That was it! I had found my purpose." In that moment, she knew that her mission was "to connect people to people and people to ideas and opportunities."

At the time, Janice was working at a dotcom she had cofounded called Total New York. She realized that the moments she was really "in-flow" were when she was working on projects that helped to connect people.

Starting a company that fully realized her mission took Janice a few more years. In 1997, her company was acquired by another, and then that company was bought by America Online. After working at AOL for a year, she knew she needed to live by her mission.

Janice brainstormed for months and finally came up with five possible businesses she could start that would help fulfill her mission.

She e-mailed the five ideas to over 500 people she had met over the years and asked their opinion about which idea seemed to be the most viable business opportunity.

The response was that she should start a company based on unique partnership ceremonies, and soon after, Love-Track.com was born. The scope of the site grew to encompass the entire relationship life cycle with the main focus being connecting people with relationship coaches.

In April 2000, there was a downturn in the Internet market and as funding began to dry up, Janice knew her company had to generate more revenue. She evolved her business into being a top source for personal, corporate, and executive coaching and Love-Track.com became Coaching Circles.

Janice advises, "Find your purpose and live it. To find it and to live it, you do not need to go at it alone. Hook up with other entrepreneurs, colleagues, and peers. Hook up with friends, family, and neighbors. Hook up with coaches and all the people around you to assist in living your full potential and purpose. This is not a selfish act. I firmly believe if we all lived our purpose, this world would be a much better place—and we'd all win."

A MOTTO FOR YOUR MISSION

A mission or vision statement can take the form of a personal motto. It is short, catchy, and easy to remember. Here are two women's stories about the origins of their mottos.

Isole Development's president and founder, Jill Harrison's motto is "Success is the only option."

Jill developed her motto before her business became financially successful, at a time when she owed enough money to make it impossible to walk away. Her motto has not changed throughout the growth of her business, and she even has it posted on her computer monitor as a daily reminder.

Jill believes in what she does and her motto sucinctly summarizes the essence of what business means to her. She realizes that every businessperson has to do what it takes to be successful, which could mean changing strategy, plan, or product. But Jill believes that changing one's will to succeed is definitely not an option.

Cofounder and vice president of Public Relations, LH3, Inc., Donna Crafton's motto is "It's all about me." Some people might think her motto is arrogant, but she believes the statement has a deeper meaning and incredible power.

Donna's motto came about when she worked in the publicity department for a major fashion designer. There, she and her girlfriends joked about how those in the fashion scene were "all about themselves." Their joke became "now back to me," referring to the inevitable phenomenon that occurred as one person listened to another person. Rather than inquiring further, they would always bring the conversation back to themselves. Donna morphed the phrase "now back to me" into "it's all about me."

Saying or thinking "it's all about me" makes Donna feel empowered, regardless of the reaction from others. "Nearly every day I reaffirm my commitment to this statement—it just applies and rings true so often for me." Even her friends have admitted that by living by the motto "it's all about me," Donna has shown she is committed not only to herself but also to them because they are important parts of her life. By being true to herself, she can then be true to the people and work that is important to her.

BUSINESS MISSIONS GET PERSONAL

As you can see from the earlier examples, women often create company mission statements that clearly reflect their personal missions. Personally, I labored each year while running Cybergrrl, Inc., to craft and update a company mission statement that truly reflected a mission I could embrace.

Cybergrrl, Inc.'s, original mission statement was:

> *To capture the mindshare of women and girls by being the premiere builder of online communities and the creator of interactive content, entertainment, and destinations that make Cybergrrl a virtual part of their entry online and an integrated part of their everyday lives.*

The mission statement finally became:

> *"To Empower Women Through Technology"*

Even today, several years after leaving the company, that business mission statement still applies to what I do every day—writing and speaking about technology and the Internet, particularly as a powerful tool for women's personal and professional lives.

Here's another example of a woman whose company mission is in line with her personal mission.

Many mission statements are developed over time and incorporate past experiences and lessons. For Debbie Tompkins, founder and president of Tompkins Benefit Group, quitting her "dream job" was the first step to formulating her mission.

At the age of 26, Debbie accepted a position as a disability brokerage manager with a national insurer, a great opportunity for a young female professional at the time. In fact, she was the first female the company had hired. Within three months of starting the job, she was frustrated and demoralized. She was told that to be successful, she had to play the hierarchical game and disregard teaching, creativity, affiliation, and fairness. She quit her "dream job" without any future prospects but felt that she had to or lose who she was.

Now in her mid-40s, Debbie looks back and feels that quitting her brokerage management job at 26 was only the first of many decisions she made to be true to herself and to honor the contributions she could make to others. It was the beginning of her mission. She admits, however, at the time she didn't really know what she was going to do. She only sensed there was more important work she could be doing.

Another example of Debbie's commitment to being true to herself and her mission happened when she was 35 and running her own business, Tompkins Benefit Group. Her family, who did not support her entrepreneurial endeavors, told her that her role as a business owner was wrong and she should find a job as someone else's secretary. They gave her an ultimatum: either quit the path she was on—running and growing a business—or they would disinherit her. Debbie chose disinheritance and although it alienated her from her family, she felt she had made the right decision.

Debbie lives by this personal mission: "To make decisions and take actions in my personal and professional life that are designed to act towards the greater good."

Staying true to her mission is accomplished in several ways. First, she does not base her decisions on money. For example, if a client is operating unethically, she focuses on doing the right thing and not on the income the business will lose if she walks away from the account.

Second, and most important to Debbie, is having a private place to get away from business to contemplate and find her way "back to center." There are times when she might get off track, and she has to remind herself to get away.

Third, her friends are critical. Debbie takes time away with friends—those not associated with her business—to provide balance to that "tsunami wave" that she sees everyone riding in the business world.

Debbie's company mission is written as if spoken to a client and includes the following four points:

1. Help you make decisions that are good for your company.
2. Build a long-term, proactive relationship with you.
3. Simplify the complex world of benefits.
4. Provide you with understandable solutions.

Debbie also identified her company's core values as part of creating a clear vision for the way she and her team conduct business:

1. We operate ethically for ethical clients.
2. We put the client first, always.
3. We adapt as necessary to meet new market challenges and continue to offer the best service and products to our clients.
4. The highest degree of confidentiality is a guiding principal in all matters regarding the client, the client's employees, and the Tompkins Benefit Group.

Debbie's clarity of mission and vision was honored by her husband when he purchased a small card that he felt summarized what was important to her. The card sits on her desk at work listing the following items:

Passion

Comprehension

Listen hard

Optimal performance

Desire

Achieve the impossible

Nap with delight

No regret

LIVE LOUDLY

FORMULATING YOUR MISSION

Coming up with a mission statement takes a deep understanding of the things you want in life—not just in business, but in your whole life.

Caroline Carmagnol, CEO of Alize Public Relations, came up with the following list of desires for every aspect of her life.

- To balance professional and private life without jeopardizing my desire for challenging positions.
- To contribute to the world by setting up a [work] structure with flexibility and a challenging but not fierce environment.
- To work with individuals I appreciate and [with whom I] share the same values.
- To realize my family is worth more than any well-paid job.
- To have new challenges.
- To focus on helping European high-tech companies successfully enter the American markets by being a perfect interface between both worlds.

- To share my time between Europe and the United States, two places I love and need in order to blossom.
- To run a [business] structure with the philosophy I have developed.
- To be independent.
- To start a [business] structure from scratch after having represented lots of start-ups, and instead, be part of the adventure of a start-up.
- To transfer my expertise and to see individuals grow.

Caroline took her list and started her own business in August 1998 with the idea of providing the women who worked for her the flexibility they deserved in order to maintain a balance between their professional and private lives. Her only request to her employees was that the job be done and the clients be well served. To Caroline, it didn't matter where the job was done as long as it was done well and on time.

Writing a business plan in order to identify the elements of a business is one way Caroline believes you can be true to your personal mission and fulfill your dreams.

"Once you have clearly outlined your philosophy, your expertise will [help you] fill in your business plan very easily," says Caroline. "If you need to make adjustments from a business standpoint, try to stick to your inner philosophy since it is, and will remain, the heart of your business and the main reason for you being where you are today: in charge!"

PERSONAL PROJECT #1:

MAKE YOUR MOTTO

Creating a motto that articulates your personal mission is like taking the project on Life Story Titles in Chapter 1 a step further. Instead of summarizing events in your life, you are looking to either sum up how you live your life or how you want to live your life—an inner belief or tenet that you believe in firmly and completely.

Your motto must be catchy, easy to say, easy to remember, and meaningful. And all of those qualities have to fit into one sentence, preferably not a run-on sentence. Think soundbite. Think short and sweet. And yes, you're allowed to "adopt" an existing motto and make it your own, as long as you take it seriously and strive to live by it.

Here are some sample mottos:

- *"Live life to its fullest."*
- *"Act with intent."*
- *"Make time for me each day."*
- *"Trust my gut."*
- *"Never kick myself when I'm down."*
- *"My work must be compatible with my heart."*
- *"Stop and smell the roses."*

Once you have your motto, you can do the following with it:

- *Use it as the screen saver on your computer.*
- *Have it printed in a stylish font on good paper, frame it and hang it on your office wall.*
- *Make buttons with your motto on it and give them away to friends, family, and colleagues at work. And wear one yourself!*
- *Handwrite it on fancy paper, roll it up, put it in a bottle with a good seal, then toss it into the ocean. Include your e-mail address and see if you ever hear from someone who finds it.*
- *Print the logo on T-shirts. Give as gifts and keep a few for yourself to wear at every appropriate occasion.*
- *Have it engraved on metal or stone or burned into wood to hang on your wall or keep on your desk as a paperweight.*

Whatever creative idea you have for displaying your motto, make sure it is something you'll actually do quickly after you've come up with it. If everything else seems too time-intensive, simply print it out and hang it on your refrigerator or give it to your kids to decorate for you. Your motto should be like a mantra –say it to yourself often and it will give you focus and direction.

PERSONAL PROJECT #2:

BUSINESS PLAN FOR YOUR LIFE

When you are writing a business plan for your business, you are forced to think about what you truly want your business to be over the next five years and beyond. Try an experiment and write a "business plan" for your life based on the elements of a traditional business plan. Here's how to get started:

- *Your Vision.* This should be an overview of the "big picture" vision for what you want to achieve in your life—not the fine details of how you will get there, but the ultimate goal.
- *Your Mission.* This should be the motto you live by. Your mission should directly support your vision but be more of an action statement than a "big-picture" view.
- *The Team.* Start with yourself. Describe your accomplishments and strengths and why you've got what it takes to accomplish your mission. If there are others who are closely involved in your life, such as a partner or spouse, add them to this section and list their strengths and how they, too, will help you reach your mission.
- *Market Summary.* This should evaluate outside conditions, situations, events, or resources that will help you reach your mission. Include what you are doing professionally and activities

you participate in that directly help you to achieve your mission. Check this section over carefully once you are finished and cut out anything that does not directly serve your mission.

- *Competition.* Define the outside people, forces, and situations that hold you back from achieving your mission. Outline how you will overcome each one to get back on track.
- *Goals and Objectives.* State your goals over a one-, three-, or five-year plan, listing steps you need to take or milestones you need to reach to achieve those goals. State specific objectives and briefly outline the resources and timeframe involved in reaching those objectives.
- *Financial Plan.* Create a cash-flow analysis of your living expenses. What extra expenses will you have to incur to achieve your goals? How will you bring in additional revenue or where can you cut down on current expenses to accommodate new ones?
- *Risks and Rewards.* Summarize the risks of undertaking your Business Plan for Life and how you will address them. Outline the rewards you will gain from pursuing this plan.
- *Key Issues.* This should be a list where you can check off each completed task that gets you closer to your mission.
- *Conclusion.* Summarize your plan, restate your mission, and give yourself some words of encouragement.

Print out your Business Plan for Life, get it bound at a local copy shop, and set it by your night table for bedtime reading. Have a pen handy so you can jot down new thoughts and ideas that come to you. Revisit your Business Plan for Life each month to see how you've progressed.

POWERTOOL 6 CHECKLIST

Make a Personal Mission Statement

- *Having a personal mission statement or vision statement or a personal motto can put into focus what you want and how you'll get it.*
- *Make sure your business mission is compatible with your personal mission.*
- *Write your mission down, read it often, say it out loud.*
- *Write a Business Plan for Life. You've spent so much time writing one for your business; now you deserve just as much attention, if not more.*

NUGGETS

BOOKS ON BUSINESS PLANS

Anatomy of a Business Plan: A Step-by-Step Guide to Starting Smart, Building the Business and Securing Your Company's Future; Linda Pinson, Dearborn Trade, 2001

The One Page Business Plan: Start With a Vision, Build a Company, James T. Horan Jr., Jim Horan, Rebccca S. Shaw, eds., One Page Business Plan Co., 1998

The Successful Business Plan: Secrets and Strategies, Rhonda M. Abrams and Eugene Kleiner, Running R Media, 2000

Your First Business Plan: A Simple Question and Answer Format Designed to Help You Write Your Own Plan, Joseph Covello, Brian J. Hazelgren, Sourcebooks Trade, 1998

WEB SITES ON BUSINESS PLANS

Bplans.com
   www.bplans.com

SBA: Starting Your Business: Business Plans
    www.sba.gov/starting/indexbusplans.html
About.com Entrepreneurs
    www.entrepreneurs.about.com/smallbusness/entrepreneurs/cs/
    businessplans

Chapter 7

BE A MENTOR

Take Time to Teach and Be a Role Model

"You cannot hope to build a better world without improving the individuals. To that end, each of us must work for his own improvement, and at the same time, share a general responsibility for all humanity, our particular duty being to aid those to whom we think we can be most useful."

—Madame Curie

L ISA KRUSS, PRESIDENT AND CEO, INTERNET PRESENCE CONSULTING, Inc., feels there are so many roles she plays in life: woman, daughter, sister, girlfriend, boss, athlete, friend. And she absolutely does see herself as a role model.

"I take the 'role' [in role model] seriously because I believe that everybody who engages in human interaction is considered a role model by others, whether or not their actions are outstanding, morally correct, or even honorable."

Adds Lisa, "We have to make the conscious effort to remind ourselves that others do pay attention to our actions, whether they acknowledge it verbally or not. Being a role model requires an enormous sense of discipline and confidence, and the belief that what you do matters. That it really matters."

Acknowledging yourself as a role model is one step closer to taking the time to be a mentor to someone else. Then you have to take the time.

IN SEARCH OF ROLE MODELS

Because the media doesn't always do justice to covering women in business, many businesswomen are hard-pressed to find role models that relate directly to their industry. Finding a woman who helmed a major technology company was impossible in 1995 and only recently possible with the rise of Carly Fiorina into the CEO position at Hewlett-Packard. Having a woman successfully leading a high-profile Internet company didn't happen until several years after I founded Cybergrrl, Inc., and such positions are still limited to a handful of women like Meg Whitman at eBay.

Whenever I'm asked who my role models have been, I half-jokingly say, "Madonna and Martha Stewart." My reasoning is that both Madonna and Martha Stewart are "living, breathing brands"—they have perfected the art of branding themselves and are doing it in "multiple media." Madonna has her music, videos, film, personal performances, and books, and Martha has books, television, products in stores, a magazine, and a web site. There is no medium they can't conquer if they try. And best of all—they are in control of their businesses and professional destinies.

MY ACCIDENTAL MENTORS

I didn't realize the value of mentors until I ended up with three, all of whom found me via e-mail.

The first one e-mailed me through my Cybergrrl.com web site asking for advice. He was concerned because his daughter was not using the computer as much as his son, and he wanted to know which web sites he could direct her to that might be interesting to her.

"How old is your daughter?" was my e-mailed reply.

"Three," he responded.

What a cool dad to be concerned about his daughter's computer use at such a young age! Via e-mail, he later offered his help and support for my business. That's when I looked at his company name and realized he was one of the most high profile New York City venture capitalists focused on the Internet industry.

We stayed in touch, and he eventually introduced my company to a friend of his who became Cybergrrl, Inc.'s, first investor.

Another e-mail arrived from a man who had just gotten off a plane where he had been reading several magazines and had come across two articles about me. He admitted he had been using the Cybergrrl logo to demo a new animation software product and had forgotten to ask permission. I gave him permission to continue using it in his demos and the software eventually became Macromedia's Flash, a successful animation program.

It also turned out he was the very first seed investor in *WiReD* magazine. His advice over the years was invaluable to me and he never failed to make time to help, including many hours on a long-distance telephone call where he went over every single page of the first draft of my company's business plan.

Around the same time, another nice e-mail message arrived from someone named Samir who complimented me on the Cybergrrl.com site and my work. I e-mailed back a "thank you" and our correspondence took off from there, mostly focusing on our business philosophies and life.

After several months of e-mailing back and forth, a message arrived that read, "I'm going to be in town. Do you want to meet for dinner?" We made arrangements to meet, picked a restaurant, and set a time. Then, finally, I realized I didn't know who to look for at the restaurant. "Are you a man or a woman?" was my next e-mail.

"A man," was the response, sent, most likely with amusement. Samir turned out to be the CEO of a Web design software company that was later purchased by IBM for a nice sum. He also was one of the wisest and most fascinating people I had ever met. His entire philosophy for business was based around infusing your heart, soul, and vision into business.

SEARCHING FOR A FEMALE MENTOR

After several years of running my Internet company and having three wonderful, male mentors, I realized there were aspects of running a business that were different as a woman. I had read about and met a businesswoman—Patrice Tanaka—who owned and ran a marketing firm that had been dubbed the "marketing company with soul."

Her office was friendly and comfortable yet efficient, with brightly colored walls and even a meditation room. Her clients were often cause-oriented organizations and companies for women. I wrote Patrice a letter—not an e-mail—asking if she would be my mentor.

She called immediately upon receiving the letter and said yes. We met soon after in her conference room over lunch and talked about the origins of our businesses and what we envisioned for them. She was the first president of a company who admitted to feeling very emotional when she had to fire an employee for the first time. My male mentors had never shared this kind of vulnerability with me. Finally, I had a mentor who could relate to issues unique to businesswomen.

E-MENTORING AS AN OPTION

Early in my career, I didn't perceive myself as a role model, nor did I give much thought to being a mentor. When you aren't certain of your abilities and haven't found the right path, you are often too busy trying to figure things out for yourself to think about how you can affect or help others.

As Cybergrrl grew and the media wrote about it, I felt the responsibility to project the most positive image of a woman at the helm of a company, a woman in the Internet industry. The pressure I put on myself was enormous and, it seemed, the expectations placed on me by the media and industry were even bigger. At that moment, I made the decision to be a positive role model and to use media coverage as a way to instruct and inspire others.

Responding to every single e-mail I received in a helpful and constructive way became a major goal. E-mail was such a fast and efficient way to reach out and touch many people's lives. To this day, e-mail remains the most effective way I mentor dozens of women at a time.

On a less technical scale, my writing and speaking engagements were also ways to reach people and hopefully influence them in a positive way. By accepting myself as a role model, foibles and all, I realized that others could learn from my successes as well as my fears and failures.

Being open, honest, and forthright about your own journey to entrepreneurship and building the business that gives you the life you love, you can lead through example and be a positive influence on other women. Business life isn't always easy, but it is a lesson-filled ride. Often the lowest moments lead us to our most powerful lessons. Don't be afraid to share those lessons when you mentor.

THE ART OF MENTORING

What are the qualities of a good mentor? According to Jennifer Floren, president and CEO of experience.com, Inc., a role model is someone who "leads by example, with self-confidence, self-respect, and most importantly, with the understanding that being a role model isn't about telling someone what to do, or what career path to take. Instead, [it is about] listening to what their goals and needs are, even if they may be different than your own."

Jennifer believes it is not just the "protégé" who benefits from a mentoring relationship, but that the careers and lives of all of the people involved in that relationship are enhanced. For example, she says, a woman with 25 years experience can benefit from hearing the fresh perspective of a younger professional who might inspire her to continue to advance her career or maybe revisit her goals.

Jennifer also feels that as a mentor guides a protégé through career choices, she benefits from her own instruction because the very act of leadership can help restore passion for her work. Says Jennifer, "Mentoring is a chance to learn from others, to connect, to share experiences, and to improve life, both in and out of the office."

Even with everything women have achieved, Jennifer does not believe the importance of young women having role models and mentors has declined. She explains that "while women should be proud of their progress in the business world—there are exceptional women in every industry, in every profession—we must also recognize that future generations of women still need guidance."

Some salient tips from Jennifer on how to become a mentor include:

- Find out if your company sponsors a mentorship program. If they do not, talk to your human resources director about establishing one. (If you run your own business, think about starting one.)

- Join a women's business organization that holds monthly events. Such an organization will provide you with a venue to develop relationships with professional women of all levels.
- Investigate opportunities at national mentoring organizations.
- Develop a relationship with a co-worker who is at a different career level than you are. Share ideas and gain perspective from her different outlook on the company, the industry and current events.
- Foster an acute awareness of the differences among the levels in your company. While you may understand that all of the company's employees are busy, do you know what they are busy with? Understanding your co-worker's job, whether she is working above or below you, will allow you to lead or follow in a more appropriate manner.

Adds Jennifer, "It has traditionally been more difficult for women to find role models, perhaps because many of our mothers, aunts, and grandmothers have not experienced the unique issues that face women in the business world today. And while there are many men who are wonderful role models, it would be remiss not to acknowledge the unique set of issues that face women in the workplace—and it is that perspective that truly can change the course of a woman's career."

INFLUENCING OTHERS

Lutchansky Communications president Robin Lutchansky mentors several women about their businesses or changing careers. She has helped many women make successful transitions, including one woman who was working as a secretary even though she had a college degree. Robin told her she was in the wrong field and helped her get involved with marketing through the American Marketing Association. Today, the woman is an investor relations executive with a dramatically enhanced net worth.

Robin's approach to mentoring is more holistic than just giving business advice. "To be a mentor, remember the whole person. The things that stop many women from being successful often have nothing to do with their intelligence or education or experience. Most times, it is emotional issues," explains Robin. "I find that what many women need or want is a guide—a guide who can teach them the logistics of business and give emotional support as needed, something most professional organizations in the mentoring field completely ignore."

THE VALUE OF MENTORS

For Gwen McIvor, president of the BridgeLight Group, a mentor was a friend who offered advice at the right moments and was there to support her at every step as she started her own business. Her friend Barbara planted the seed for Gwen's business concept a year before the company was actually launched.

Barbara, who was a successful entrepreneur, began to prod and encourage Gwen to go out on her own and "ditch the corporate world." Gwen remembers Barbara commenting that she was certain Gwen had the rare combination of personality, skills, and expertise it would take to be successful. Gwen admits that there have been few people in her life who have expressed so much faith in her and that it was a tremendous motivator.

However, it wasn't until she was laid off from her job at a high-tech company that Gwen began on the course of becoming a full-time entrepreneur. "The day I was let go, my first stop was Barbara's house for a hot cup of herbal tea, graham crackers, and a shoulder," says

Gwen. "Barbara has never let up on her faith in me and has offered countless hours of support, sound business advice, marketing ideas, and nudges to keep me moving forward when I needed it."

As Gwen approaches the first year anniversary of her business, she knows there is no going back. As her mentor, Barbara not only shared her business savvy with Gwen but gave her emotional support as well.

"The best mentoring relationships evolve over time," says Debbie Bernard, president of Bernard Marketing Associates, who has had an ongoing mentoring relationship with the vice president of her company, Lissa Heaton. "In some of the better scenarios I've seen, the mentor is a boss who likes you and takes you under his or her wing. They help groom you, and teach you on a day-to-day basis. They sit down and take the time to show you the real details that help you learn. The most important role of the mentor is to take the time to explain things."

Debbie supervised Lissa when both were in the marketing department of a home builder. Lissa was right out of college, marketing degree in hand, but had no on-the-job experience. She admits it was hard to get a job straight out of school, but Debbie saw something in her and gave her a chance to learn and grow.

Debbie explains that what she saw in Lissa from their first meeting was an ability to listen, to focus, and to absorb what Debbie said to her, indicating that Lissa would be a good learner and great to work with. When Debbie left the company where they both worked and started her own business, she knew Lissa would be on her team.

Some of the things Lissa has learned from Debbie have been gleaned through observation. "It's great to see how Debbie deals with customers, clients, and employees, and how she can adapt to different people in her conversations," says Lissa. "Watching her motivate people is very helpful. Being with her all the time and listening to her, I've had the benefit of all of her experience. Now, when I need to make a decision, I ask myself, 'how would Debbie handle this situation?' If your mentors are knowledgeable and experienced, and have established a great name for themselves, you can't go wrong."

Debbie believes good mentors open doors, especially for those in the early stages of their career. A mentor lets you grow and watches out for you. In terms of being a good mentor, Debbie advises you to "go with your gut, always be clear about where you want to be going, keep the creative juices flowing, that is, don't let familiarity mean stagnation, and challenge each other gently."

PERSONAL PROJECT #1:

FIND A MENTOR

If you do not have a mentor but have always thought it would be great to have one, now is the time to find one. To prepare for finding and getting a mentor, take care of a few things first:

- Decide what role you want your mentor to play in your life. Will they answer financial questions or advise you on employee issues? Will they introduce you to potential clients or refer you to vendors they use and trust? Are you expecting them to be like a personal coach? If so, maybe you should hire a personal coach instead.

- Set realistic parameters for tapping into your mentor's time. Are you looking for someone to speak with several times a day? Chances are this is a role for a spouse, best friend, or family member, and that much demand, even on their time, could be detrimental. A weekly check-in for half an hour is more manageable. If your mentor is high-profile or time-constrained, a 15-minute monthly check-in may be more in order.

- Define the mentoring setting. Will you be mentored via e-mail which is fast, efficient, and convenient? Or will you sit down once a month for a two-hour lunch? Or will you be mentored by phone? Create the most appealing setting for both you and your mentor.

How do you find a mentor? Here are a few places to look:

- Your family.
- Your friends.
- Your business colleagues.
- Someone you've met at church or an organization to which you belong.
- Someone you've met at a business networking event who you admire.
- Someone you've read about in the business section of your local paper who is doing something you'd like to know more about.
- Mentoring programs, particularly with national or local professional organizations.

How do you approach someone to be your mentor?

- Ask them in person, on the phone, via e-mail, or in a letter. When you ask, briefly outline your expectations and their time commitment, then let them help you shape the form of the relationship.
- Ask for an introduction from a mutual friend or acquaintance and have the person making the introduction explain why you would like to meet them.

No matter how you choose to "pop the question," make sure you put your ideas for the ideal mentoring relationship in writing so you can hand or send them a one-page document with a concise plan. This way you are ensuring your intent and expectations are clear. Then stick with the parameters you both set so as not to take advantage of your mentor or abuse your relationship with her or him.

The mentor/protégé relationship can be a delicate balance and should always be positive and beneficial for both parties.

PERSONAL PROJECT #2:

BE A MENTOR

So you want to be a mentor? Arranged with thought and care, you will find the mentoring experience rewarding and inspiring. Don't be surprised if you learn as much, if not more, than your protégé.

While there are often many resources for finding a young girl to mentor including non-profit organizations and schools, finding another woman to mentor can sometimes be a little more challenging.

You can find a protégé in a variety of places and situations. Your potential protégé could be:

- A member of your staff at your business.
- Someone you have met at a business networking event.
- A recent college graduate entering the workplace.
- A family member, friend, or business associate.
- Someone in need, such as a woman in a homeless shelter or domestic violence shelter.

Be open to mentoring. Tell people that you are looking for some-one to mentor. Once you spread the word you'll find that there is not a dearth of protégés. Your challenge will be to narrow down the candidates to choose the right one for you.

Clearly outline why you want to be a mentor. Then define how much time you are willing to give and the most convenient manner in which you can impart your wisdom.

E-mail and phone are less time-consuming if you set limits, but sitting down in person with someone can be the most rewarding since you can literally watch your protégé's progress over time. Whatever you decide is the best way for you to mentor, make sure you stick to your commitment. If you are afraid to make a long-term commitment, offer twice a month for three months. The results of mentoring do not come overnight, so do not expect instant gratification.

As a mentor, establish boundaries and keep the relationship on a professional level. Yes, your protégé may become your friend, but never lose sight of why you began the relationship. At some point you may make a mutual decision to be just friends instead of mentor and protégé.

Overall, being a mentor is a wonderful way to pass on your knowledge and the wisdom you have gained through the years. Even if you are new at running a business, there is someone else out there who hasn't even started a business but wants to. Already, you have a wealth of information and experience, so don't ever feel you have nothing to offer. Share your knowledge.

POWERTOOL 7 CHECKLIST
Be a Role Model, Be a Mentor

- *Whether you know it or not, you are a role model to someone else. Live each moment as if someone is watching you, looking up to you and learning from you.*

- *Take the time to mentor someone else, even if it is on the telephone or through e-mail. Your time can make a difference in someone else's career and life.*
- *If you don't already have one, identify a mentor for yourself and ask if they will mentor you.*
- *The best mentoring relationships are those that are clearly defined by both parties in advance and that are mutually beneficial. One-sided mentoring isn't enough.*

NUGGETS

BOOKS ON MENTORING

Be Your Own Mentor: Career Strategies for Women, Shelia Wellington and Betty Spence (contributor), Random House, 2001

Making Mentoring: A Simple and Effective Guide to Implementing a Successful Mentoring Program, Kathy Lacey, Business and Professional Pub, 2000

The Mentor's Guide: Facilitating Effective Learning Relationships, Lois J. Zachary, Jossey-Bass, 2000

Mentoring Heroes: 52 Fabulous Women's Paths to Success and the Mentors Who Empowered Them, Mary K. Doyle, 3E Press, 2000

WEB SITES ON MENTORING

Learning Mentors (articles/resources)
 www.fastcompany.com/online/resources/learnment.html

Women's Ways of Mentoring (article)
 www.fastcompany.com/online/17/womentoring.html

SBA Mentoring: Women's Network for Entrepreneurial Training Mentoring Program (WNET)
 www.sbaonline.sba.gov/womeninbusiness/wnet.html

Chapter 8

NURTURE YOUR NETWORK

Cultivate It and It Will Nourish You

"Women, when describing their roles in their organizations, usually referred to themselves as being in the middle of things. Not at the top, but in the center; not reaching down, but reaching out."

—**Sally Helgesen**

WHEN SALLY MEECHAM, FOUNDER AND CEO OF TRAVELDONKEY Limited, first went to stores to find books about starting an Internet business, she couldn't find any. "When I founded my company in January 2000, I had never worked within the Internet [industry]. I did not have any contacts or friends within the industry, and it was all a bit daunting."

To break into networking, Sally began going to meetings for local women's business organizations, attending about three per week. At first, going to the events scared her, but she knew they were essential for the growth of her business.

Networking events have proven to be invaluable for Sally. "You find out quickly what other events are going on at each event [you attend]. I have not only made excellent contacts for partnerships, affiliates, and funding, but I have made some excellent personal friends. Ten months later, I am now even speaking at these events; it is most definitely an accelerated learning process and can quite often be a lot of fun."

DISCOVERING NETWORKING

In 1994, while I was not yet an entrepreneur but an executive director for a domestic violence awareness nonprofit organization, I attended my first conference for women in business organized by American Women's Economic Development (AWED) in New York City.

In the morning, I sat in on a workshop about networking. Although following up and staying in touch is easy for me, especially with e-mail, attending networking events and trying to make fruitful contacts with total strangers has always gripped my heart in a fist of fear. My networking event tactic has been to stand by the food table so two things happen: (1) People have to walk over to me (the food); (2) We immediately have something in common to start up a conversation (the food).

Sitting in the session on networking, I was awestruck by the workshop leader. Her name was Lucy Rosen, and she was a living, breathing, walking Rolodex. In between her advice on networking, she would ask people in the audience what they did and what they needed. Most of them needed new clients or other specific help with their business, and she proceeded to rattle, off the top of her head, the names and phone numbers of at least two or three people to contact for each one of their needs.

"I want to be just like her," I thought as I watched Lucy, the ultimate networker. After the first session, unable to muster the courage to speak with her, I did the next best thing. I followed her around the conference until she went to her next session, then sat in the back of the room to listen, hoping she didn't notice me "stalking" her.

For another 45 minutes, she continued her superhuman referral process, glancing only once at her address book for a phone number. After the session, she told me about a networking group she had formed called "Women on the Fast Track." I decided to join the group and vowed to myself that someday, I would be a networking queen, just like Lucy Rosen. I joined her networking group, which focused on bringing specific leads to other members of the group as a way of networking and supporting one another. This form of active networking was a revelation for me.

NETWORKING, MY WAY

These days, I've made it my personal project to amass a large, loose network of people with a diverse set of skills, experiences, and businesses and "hook people up" often, that is, make e-mail introductions between people who should know one another.

Sometimes, the matchmaking I do comes from e-mailed requests for my help. When unable to help directly, I always know at least one other person who can. Other times, its simply knowing that if Person A met Person B, they'd have a lot in common and could end up doing business together, so I make the intro.

Why network? Part of your motivation could be a sense of accomplishment when your matches pay off, and you get that "thank you" e-mail that proves your instincts were right. And part of your motivation could be purely selfish, because the more referrals you make that work out, the more people you have brought into your closer, more personal network. Those people become the ones who you can call on for favors and help when you need it.

Selfish? I use that word in the most positive sense—because fundamentally the building of your network is for you and for your business. Building your network, however, should not be done selfishly. When you meet someone, don't think, "What can they do for me?," but instead, "What can I do for them?" The benefits of this approach will pay off immensely when you need something.

NETWORKING ACCORDING TO LUCY ROSEN

I'm sure once you hear Lucy Rosen, president of The Business Development Group, Inc., talk about networking in her own words, you'll see how and why she has greatly influenced my own theories about networking.

QUESTION: *How have you used your network to benefit your own company?*

LUCY: I have what I call an "Inside Circle of 12." These are 12 people (entrepreneurs or people who work in companies) who know me and my business so well that they can sell my services as well as I do. They know my markets, they know who I want to target, they know what services my company provides, and they are my "rainmakers." These relationships have been cultivated very carefully and have taken over a dozen years to really develop. My network brings me business effortlessly. I don't do cold calls. I don't do advertising. Ninety-nine percent of my business comes from my entire network that is much more vast than the 12 mentioned, but those are my "inside circle."

QUESTION: *What is your philosophy on building and using your network?*

LUCY: "Gotta keep workin' it." It's not enough to go to an event and hand out business cards. It's not enough to go to one meeting and expect business from the people you meet. You've got to enter a networking relationship like a dating relationship: you've got to take time to get to know the person and cultivate the relationship. Let it grow, let it build.

Also, a lot of people say they "network" but in fact they are in it to "take." If you are a taker, you are not a networker. You have to be as willing to give as to receive. Giving is 80 percent of the networking process. You should be the first one to offer up some information or a contact. You should be the one to take the first step without expectation of a return. This is the way the process starts.

QUESTION: *Who are some of the key players in your network and how do they help you?*

LUCY: Other people in business: accountants, attorneys, printers, designers, all people who are in business and basically at the same level [my company is at] in terms of growth. I also have staff members that are terrific networkers. They know my philosophy, and adhere to the principles of giving—they bring in some of our best clients.

QUESTION: *What advice do you have for other entrepreneurs about nurturing their network?*

LUCY: There are six things to remember:
1. Be generous with your information and contacts. Don't keep score, but also know how to stop if it turns out to be a one-way street.
2. Don't expect anything overnight. It is a process and takes time.
3. Know what you do. A lot of people don't even know how to introduce themselves properly and to succinctly say who they are and what they do. No one wants to hear a story. Say it short and sweet.
4. Actively listen for pieces of information that would be beneficial for others and share it with them.
5. Follow up! It doesn't do any good to meet someone, take their card, and then never call them. Call and meet with them. Offer them something.

6. Ask people that you meet what you can do to help them be a success. What do they need? What do they want? Who do they need to meet?

THE NEED/GIVE PHILOSOPHY

In 1995, I put my own networking approach into action by founding a global networking group—Webgrrls International—to help women learn about and use the Internet for their professional lives.

In April 1995, e-mails to several women online led to a meeting at an Internet café with six women sitting around a computer terminal, talking about their mutual interest in the Web. We agreed to meet again the following month, same time, same place, and at each monthly meeting, attendance more than doubled. By November 1995, 200 women came to the New York City meeting. Meanwhile, women began meeting under the Webgrrls name in cities around the world, including Seattle, Washington; Wellington, New Zealand; Sydney, Australia; Toronto, Canada; and San Francisco, California.

As Webgrrls continued to grow as an organization, making sure the local meetings were productive was important, so I asked each woman attending to stand up and tell us the following things:

- Who you are
- What you do
- What you need from the group
- What you can give back to the group

The above process was similar to what Lucy Rosen had developed for "Women on the Fast Track," but in a much larger setting.

In my mind, the four questions accomplished the following:

1. Women identified themselves in front of the group so that others knew who they were.
2. Women talked about themselves. I had observed that many women shy away from talking about what they do and have accomplished, especially in front of other people. I wanted women to feel comfortable standing up in front of a crowd and talking about themselves.
3. Women asked for help. I think women are inclined to give to and help others before they ever ask for help themselves. I wanted to force women to first ask for what they needed. No fears, no guilt.
4. Women could offer help if they wanted. I suggested that the women in the meeting probably knew or had something that would be valuable to others even though they might not yet realize it. And I emphasized not to feel guilty if they didn't know how to immediately help.

The great thing about the Need/Give process was that once the "formal networking" was finished, women knew exactly who they wanted to speak with further. Every woman was identified, her skills and experience as well as her needs were known, and everyone could meet and match up with as many people as they wanted in a more directed way. Business partnerships were formed, consultants found clients, and Webgrrls members found jobs, advice, and help.

Isn't that what successful networking is all about?

NETWORKING IN ACTION

Meeting people is not the most important part of networking. Knowing how to cultivate and leverage your network is what successful networking is all about.

President and founder of MirrerSearch.com, Candy Mirrer's network consists of women entrepreneurs, senior executives in the technology space, and other senior executives from various industries in over 75 countries. She has used her network to generate business leads, find candidates for her recruiting company, and identify potential strategic partners.

Having spent more than 20 years working abroad in 17 countries, Candy has kept in touch with her contacts, which has led to additional contacts. She also attends networking meetings for women in business, including Women in Technology Inc., Forum for Women Entrepreneurs, Women in Development, Global Business Association, and the World Economic Forum.

Before e-mail, Candy wrote letters to stay in touch with her contacts in other parts of the world, particularly in places such as Sri Lanka where telecommunications systems weren't optimal. For the past six years, she has used a combination of e-mail, voice mail, telephone conversations, and faxes as her networking tools.

Candy says she has generally not been afraid to approach people, but admits it does take practice. She learned to refine her approach and even began to better understand who to contact to be more targeted in her networking. Candy feels that intuition helps her network, but she also firmly believes that networking skills can be learned.

Says Candy, "You should give and take and not see a network as a vehicle to ask 'Do you know so and so because I need to speak with them.' People should see networks as building communities and relationships."

> ### E-QUOTE: KATHLEEN ZEMAITIS,
> ### PRESIDENT AND FOUNDER, ZINE COMMUNICATIONS
>
> *"Building networks is easy, but may be intimidating to women because it involves a lot of cold calling, handshaking, giving out business cards, and talking about yourself. For some reason, I have found that men are more at ease with this process of self-promotion. They feel it's the nature of business. Women feel they're being pushy. Go out there, meet people, hand out your card, and call whomever you want. The worst people could do is give you the cold shoulder. Then so be it, but at least you've tried to make a connection."*

CREATING NETWORK CIRCLES

Think of your network as a series of concentric circles. The outer circle—let's call it CIRCLE 5—is made up of people you meet at networking events. You don't really know them, but you have their business card and an idea of what they do. Maybe you even know what they need and have plans to help them by introducing them to someone else you know. The contacts in Circle 5 are the ones that take effort on your part to cultivate and convert into one of the inner circles.

Next is CIRCLE 4, which consists of your friends and family. Why aren't they closer to the center? The relation of friends and family to your business is a tricky one. While friends and family are an excellent network to tap into for your business, be forewarned that the connections may come with emotional strings attached.

In CIRCLE 3 are your clients. Satisfied clients are often your number one source of new client leads, but keep in mind that there is often a delicate balance in your client relationships. Not every client will feel it is appropriate for you to ask for referrals, so gauge your relationship carefully. More often than not, however, they will make referrals unsolicited by you, particularly if they are pleased with your work.

CIRCLE 2 consists of your business associates. These are people with whom you do business or have done business. Unlike with clients, you have a more flexible relationship with business associates. You should be able to easily ask anyone in Circle 2 for client leads and business contacts. And put your competitors in Circle 2. Why? Because if you have more work than you can handle, you can refer the work to a capable company with whom you already have a relationship to get a finder's fee and still be part of the client relationship.

CIRCLE 1 is your closest network. These are the select people who know you and your business almost as well as you do. Sometimes these can be your employees (like in Lucy Rosen's case), however, I'd put employees into CIRCLE 1A because you can't always turn to your employees for everything you need for your business. You should be able to talk to your Circle 1 about anything and call on them at any time.

Your CIRCLE 1 network are the people you can count on in a pinch, the ones you can trust implicitly, the people who never expect anything in return even though you both know the relationship is balanced and mutually beneficial.

CIRCLE 1 does require seeding and cultivation. Always be aware when someone in one of your outer circles shows signs of being ready to join an inner circle. And always be on the lookout for things you can do to nurture those already in Circle 1. Don't take anyone for granted.

CIRCLE 1 also requires weeding. Sometimes you may have a falling out or a drifting apart from someone in your innermost circle. Sometimes you give and give and give and get absolutely nothing in return. Weeding is simple—just stop making the effort and the contact will "expire." Or, if the relationship is important to you, take the person out to breakfast and speak openly to them about how you feel. Sometimes a misunderstanding may seem like a weed, but a little extra communication clears everything up.

Remember to tend to all of your Circles—not just Circle 1—because each one can bring unexpected value to your network, your business, and your life.

PERSONAL PROJECT #1:

NAME TAG TRICKS

Name tags can be funny things at networking events. Usually, only a person's name is printed on the tag, which is pretty meaningless in a networking situation. I always bring a thick black permanent marker to events so I can add my company name to my tag. Give it a try! You'll notice people start speaking to you more often, usually starting off with the question, "So what does your company do?"

You may also want to add a cute catch phrase or question to your tag. Write legibly and make sure your message fits on the tag. Or use an extra blank tag and wear it below your name and company name. "Ask me about Cybergrrl" always got attention for me. If Christine Harmel put "I'm a Digital Yenta" on her name tag, she'd be guaranteed a response.

Sandy Musson, president of By The Hour, Inc., owns a company that provides backup office services to small home office and start-up companies, and she always brings her own name tag to events. It is a large gold metal pin with her name engraved in easy to read letters, and pasted on it is a section of her business card with her bright, eye-catching logo.

You may want to bring one of those plastic name tag holders—the see-through plastic casing with a pin attached to the back—and slide in a different customized name tag for each event. Sometimes, when the event host misspells my name or company name yet again, I just slide my business card into one of these plastic holders. It is a little harder to read, but I know it attracts attention as people lean in to see it.

When you go to a networking event, think of yourself as a walking billboard—either you're blank, which will never bring in business, or you can leverage your name tag and attract attention wherever you go. You decide.

PERSONAL PROJECT #2:

PLAY MATCHMAKER, MATCHMAKER

Set a goal to make an introduction between two people you know or have recently met. Once a month, once a week, whatever you feel can happen based on your schedule.

Keep track of the matches you make and follow up with the "matchees" to see if anything has come from your introduction. If so, make a note about the results. You now have someone with the potential to move into one of your networking inner circles.

How do you keep track of your network matchmaking? While some people still use index cards, I highly recommend contact database software such as Act™ or Microsoft Outlook™. Many of the these software products allow you to make notes about each contact, and that is where you can record recent dealings with that person or information about an introduction you have made for them. Go through your contact database on a regular basis to see who you have met, what they need, and what you have done for them.

Does networking sound like hard work? Sure it is, but even if you pay attention to your network once a month, you will definitely reap the rewards of your efforts. Networking is a lot like gardening. Even someone with a brown thumb can learn essential skills to keep a garden of contacts alive. If you feel networking isn't your strongest skill, you can practice the techniques mentioned above, and begin to grow a network that can benefit both you and your business.

Like a garden, your network will nourish and sustain you. All it needs in return is your attention and care.

POWERTOOL 8 CHECKLIST
Nurture Your Network

- *Go into network thinking "What can I do for them?" instead of "What can they do for me?"*
- *Networking is a two-way street. If both parties aren't benefiting, cut the connection.*
- *Let your network know how much you appreciate them. The best way to do this is to keep their needs in mind as you meet other people.*
- *Keep your contact information organized.*
- *Seed and weed your contacts, that is, add new people as you meet them but also weed out those who are just taking without giving.*

NUGGETS

BOOKS ABOUT NETWORKING

Breakthrough Networking: Building Relationships That Last, Lillian D. Bjorseth, Duoforce Enterprises, 1996

Fifty-Two Ways to Reconnect, Follow-Up and Stay in Touch When You Don't Have Time to Network, Anne Baber and Lynne Waymon, Waymon and Associates, 1993

Make Your Connections Count: The Six-Step System to Build Your Meganetwork, Melissa Giovagnoli, Dearborn Trade, 1994

Power Networking: 55 Secrets for Personal and Professional Success, Donna Fisher, Sandy Vilas, Bard Press, 2000

The Secrets of Savvy Networking: How to Make the Best Connections for Business and Personal Success, Susan Roane, Warner Books, 1993

WEB SITES ABOUT NETWORKING

Five Keys to Networking Success (article)
   www.businessknowhow.com/marketing/network1.htm

About.com Career Planning (resources)
   www.careerplanning.about.com/careers/careerplanning/cs/networking/

Introduction to Networking (articles)
   www.profnet.org/report.net

Chapter 9

WIELD YOUR POWER

Revel in Your Accomplishments and Brag

"The thing women have got to learn is that nobody
gives you power. You just take it."

—**Roseanne Barr, comedienne and actress**

STEPHANIE SPENCE, HEAD OF SPENCE PUBLISHING, FEELS HER PERsonal power comes from knowing she is a role model for her daughters. "I want them to know they can have or do anything they want in this life. We have choices, yet often are fearful of which is the wrong or right choice. Take the leap and land where you land."

In terms of finding your power, Stephanie says she has learned that to be truly powerful, you must be willing to live your life on your own terms. She believes power comes from being who you are and not from copying someone else. Break the rules, do something no one else has done, and do it your way.

Be an original. Your power is your own. Revel in it.

THE TRUTH ABOUT POWER

Being comfortable with your own power and abilities may sound simplistic. Maybe you can't understand why any woman might not feel comfortable with her personal power. But think carefully about the dynamics in any business setting, particularly where men outnumber women. Is the woman always heard equally? Is the woman heard at all? If you are that woman, do you believe you have equal power in the room, equal to any of the men? Do the men feel you do?

Maybe you don't think of power based on gender or maybe you don't consider gender to be an issue as you do business. On the one hand, denying that you are "female" and assuming the role of "person" or "businessperson" can seem like the solution to being on equal footing with the men around you.

Unfortunately, denying you are a female in business diminishes your power. While you may believe you've never been discriminated against or perceived differently because you are female, most likely, it is happening in subtle ways, ways that may not be obvious to you. You'll never be "one of the guys," and you'll always be outside the real "boy's club." But don't worry. That's actually OK.

Sometimes women try so hard to either be like men or to fit in with men that they ignore what they bring to the business table as women. Instead of trying to join the "boy's club," spend more time cultivating a "girl's network." Create a powerful, supportive force within your company, industry, and community comprised of women whom you respect.

OH, IT'S NOTHING, REALLY

Too often, I've noticed that women downplay their accomplishments, diminishing their power. Where men are the first to toot their own horns, women hide the horn or stuff something into it so others can't even toot it for them. Boasting and bragging is perceived as a negative quality and unbecoming of a "lady."

In conversations with some of the women featured in this book, even when they insisted they were comfortable talking about their achievements, they were also quick to say, "I don't brag, though." Let's face it. "Talking about your achievements" is really just "bragging and boasting." Women like to think they do it more "modestly" or "less offensively." But watch out—if you are too quiet about your achievements, most people will not hear you.

As women, we tend to dilute our power because we're afraid of how other people will perceive us. Will they accept us if we are powerful individuals or powerful women? We are too often looking for ways to make our power seem more acceptable and palatable to others. Does this sound familiar?

Now don't go into a meeting or conversation and behave like a self-centered, obnoxious jerk, but do acknowledge your skills, achievements, and strengths without hesitation or embarrassment. Talking easily about your accomplishments is one way to harness your power. In the long run, you are the only one who will lose out if you fail to speak up, hold back from tooting your horn, or don't sell yourself. Your silence is someone else's opening. And your power slowly leaks away.

I'M SORRY, YOU GO AHEAD

Consider how some women behave in front of an audience. After attending many conferences and watching or participating in countless panel discussions, here is one of my main observations.

When a panel is made up of all men, they tend to talk over one another comfortably. They put in their two cents wherever and whenever they want, and they will often dominate the floor far beyond their allotted time without apology.

When the panel is made up of men and women, the men tend to dominate. They are just behaving in the manner they always do. The women on the panel, however, often wait their turn to speak, which usually means they don't get to say much. Unless the panel moderator is very good, a lone woman on any panel can actually go through the entire program without saying more than a handful of words. Even when it is her turn to speak, the men on the panel have no qualms interrupting her, and unless she is aggressive, the woman will not get the floor back. She loses her turn to speak.

When the panel is made up of just women, they are almost always too polite. They listen intently to each woman speaking, and wait their turn to speak, even if they have something to say as another woman is speaking. Sometimes, they might hesitantly raise their hand, asking for permission to speak. And if they accidentally interrupt another woman, they immediately say, "I'm sorry, you go ahead."

Now I'm not saying that the above analysis of panels is the absolute rule, and I've definitely seen powerhouse women speaking on panels who don't shrink away from being heard. However, these "panel dynamics" have happened so many times that it is impossible to ignore the pattern.

As a panelist, I have had to train myself to realize that my opinions and ideas are valid and deserve to be heard. If I'm on a panel with men, I have to charge ahead and get my words in, even if it means raising my voice. You really have to pay attention to the volume and pitch of your voice and speak more forcefully if someone cuts you off. Practice grabbing back the floor instead of waiting, waiting, waiting for the next "proper" opening. On panels with men, that polite pause rarely happens, and you could be waiting for an eternity for the "right moment" to speak.

As a moderator, I often end up with all-female panels, which at technology, Internet, and general business events, is still a rarity. My written rules for the panelists include an express request that they interrupt one another and get their two cents in wherever they want. They have my permission to complete their thought rather than leave it hanging if someone else steps in with an opinion. I also encourage them to challenge one another, disagree, and feel free to argue a point or comment on something another panelist has said.

And you know what? It doesn't always work. Only the savviest speakers seem to have the guts to follow my instructions, while the rest still wait their turn to speak. Luckily, as moderator, I can make sure everyone gets a chance to have their say and that no one dominates the floor. But it never ceases to amaze me how many women—powerful and successful businesswomen—let their "good-girl manners" get in the way of being heard, particularly in a forum where people are interested in hearing what they have to say.

Your voice is part of your power. Use it!

THE MALE/FEMALE DYNAMIC

The dynamics on panels between men and women are also evident in nearly every business setting, meeting, conference call, or discussion. When a group is mixed, men tend to dominate the conversation. I'm not passing judgment on that phenomenon—it is just their way, not good or bad.

When women get together, they have a different rhythm or style of communicating. Unlike during panel discussions in front of an audience, they can have very animated conversations, putting in their two cents freely, and interrupting each other with their thoughts. But they always have an uncanny awareness of anyone they've cut off and expertly let that other person back into the conversation.

Then, the minute a man is introduced into the mix, things suddenly change. Let's call it the "Male/Female Dynamic"—not very original but it is something that must be chemical as well as societal. The energy or the air in the room actually seems to change when testosterone meets estrogen. First, some women might turn their head to watch the man, others might squirm in their seat or begin to fuss with their hair or face. Observing the reactions in the room resembles watching animals in the wild.

When a man enters a room of women, some of the women who had very strong voices earlier are suddenly shy and reserved. Other women become resentful that the man is there, and give him dirty looks. If the man opens his mouth, unaware of the reactions around him, he may assume his "proper role" of domination and take over the conversation, assuming the floor and holding onto it. You think I'm making this up?

Recently, a new chapter leader for Webgrrls International was asking for advice about how to run her group. Then she told me "You know, I don't think I agree with the idea that only women can attend Webgrrls meetings. I don't think there's anything wrong with having men in the group." I explained to her that while Webgrrls cannot deny men the opportunity to attend meetings or join the group, the whole reason Webgrrls exists is to be a forum for women.

She insisted she still didn't understand why a forum just for women was needed. I told her about my theories on the male/female dynamic, emphasizing that I'm not against men at all, but for creating some time and space for women to network without men around. She said, "I don't believe there's a difference when men are in the room."

The irony of her statement was that only half an hour before we started our conversation, she brought me to visit some businesswomen at a nearby company. We all sat around sharing information at a large conference table at one of the women's office.

About halfway through the visit, a man walked into the room. He was the head of a major technology organization in the area and extremely supportive of Webgrrls. He began to talk about his organization and how he wanted to provide resources for Webgrrls to help the new chapter get established. Then he began to talk about the industry, people in the industry, the market, and on and on and on.

Everyone at the table listened politely, and then it was time for me to leave. As the Webgrrls chapter leader and I got into her car, she muttered under her breath, "He's a nice guy, but I wish he would have shut up for a minute."

So there we were, less than half an hour later, and she was insisting that there was no such thing as the male/female dynamic. When I recounted for her the series of events that occurred in that conference room, she was stunned. "I didn't even realize that it was happening," she admitted. And yet, subconsciously, she had felt the dynamic in the room change, it had annoyed her, and she had commented on it afterwards.

Needless to say, she now champions women-only forums as an alternative to coed forums as a place where women can have their space and find their voice.

WOMEN AND POWER

Understanding power and how to use it can take different forms for different women. It took Alexandria K. Brown, founder and president of AKB & Associates, some time to get used to the fact that she had power, or as she puts it, that she was "coming from strength."

Three of the ways Alexandria built up what she calls "her strength" were by creating reserves of money, time, and energy for herself. Even when she was worried about cash flow, she scheduled a weekly massage and dance lessons which gave her energy. Creating these "reserves" helped her feel more in control than ever before. She attracts more of what she wants—the right people, projects, and money—all because she comes from a position of strength.

Alexandria believes she has become a more confident person over the last few years. Yet she still hears that little girl voice inside saying things like, "How can you think so big? Who do you think you are, Ali Brown?" or "This client truly thinks you're an expert, but do you really know your stuff?" or "You've never done a project like this before. Perhaps it's too risky." She calls that voice "self-sabotage," and whenever she feels the voice taking over, she rereads a quote by Marianne Williamson from *A Return to Love* (HarperCollins Publishers):

> *Our worst fear is not that we are inadequate.*
> *Our deepest fear is that we are powerful beyond measure.*

When you begin to get comfortable with power, others around you will react in various ways, some positive and some negative, as Alexandria discovered. As she grew more successful according to her own standards and began to give off an aura of confidence, she noticed that some people reacted to her with jealousy, including her boyfriend of four years.

As her business grew and she was about to make more money than her boyfriend, he suddenly postponed their engagement, saying he "wasn't ready." Then he began to make little comments like, "That client will never pay your rates," and when money got tight, he would tell Alexandria that she should start looking for a job again. Alexandria knew he would never be the supportive person she needed him to be and when he finally proposed again, she declined.

When you become more comfortable with your power, you might lose some of the people who you considered friends, but you will also begin to attract more supportive people. "The friends who stick around are worth it. They want to see you at your glorious best," says Alexandria. "I'm now engaged to an amazingly supportive man who is just as ambitious and considerate as I am. His attitude is 'Go, Ali, go!' I'm surrounded by only those friends who want the best for me. Out with the old, in with the new—new friends to match the true you."

BRAG, BRAG, BRAG

Why does bragging have such a negative connotation, particularly for women? Women seem to be taught that it is not "ladylike" or "proper" to brag about one's accomplishments. Yet men rarely hesitate to make it known—in any forum or setting—what they have done and how good they are at what they do. For Alison Berke Morano, president of bworks.com, Inc., acknowledging her achievements has helped her to appreciate her own power.

All of Alison's accomplishments are written down and she mentions them a lot. They are in her sales pitch, on her web site, and even on her business cards. People tell her they are impressed with her background, and she gets hired and spotlighted because people know about her achievements. "Everyone who asks me what I've done knows that I was *Small Businessperson of the Year* in 1999, named one of Long Island's *"40 under 40,"* and served as vice president of the *Great Neck Chamber of Commerce*. They also know Hillary Rodham Clinton called once to congratulate me on my "Millennium Project" proposal for the town where I lived," says Alison.

SHE READS

Recommended by Alexandria K. Brown, Founder and President, AKB & Associates

Coach Yourself to Success by Talane Miedaner
"In this book, internationally acclaimed life coach Talane Miedaner (my personal life coach) shares her universal keys to achieving personal success. Miedaner shares 101 of her most powerful and effective coaching tips. If you buy this book and don't love it, I'll buy it back from you. Seriously!"

Good Girls Don't Get Ahead, Gutsy Girls Do by Kate White
"[White discusses] how taking chances and smart risks and being selfish in a good way can get you ahead of the pack. Example: wearing your heart (or your passion) on your sleeve can often be beneficial."

The Seven Secrets of Women Who Get Everything They Want by Kate White
"In order to stay ahead of the pack you need to take chances, risks, and be selfish. One simple example is to get used to asking for exactly what you want."

Alison insists that women need to get over being shy about their accomplishments. She points to a girlfriend who asked for some help with her résumé. Alison told her to put certain relevant achievements in bold type. "But isn't that bragging?" asked her friend. Of course it was, but she was going for a sales position, and she had to sell herself first. Later, Alison received an e-mail from her friend thanking her. The headhunter was duly impressed.

Sometimes it is easier to advise others to brag about themselves than to do it yourself. Even Alison admits there are times when she doesn't follow her own advice, but she keeps reminding herself it is OK to brag. And she also has good friends and a supportive husband to remind her in case she forgets.

Surround yourself with people who enjoy listening to you toot your horn, that is, people who are proud of your accomplishments and do not put you down for talking about them.

E-QUOTE: KIMBERLY L. MCCALL, PRESIDENT, MCCALL MEDIA AND MARKETING, INC.

"As a younger woman just starting out, I was very sensitive about power and hierarchy within the companies I worked for. I had the mistaken belief that power came with a title—so since I was a manager at 25, I thought I should automatically be respected and revered. I was so, so wrong. What I've learned is that power is much, much more subtle and nuanced than I thought. I was taking the steamroller approach, and as a woman, that just does not work.

"I think [becoming comfortable with my power] has been an evolution that comes with maturity and conviction. The more I believe in what I do, treat people well, and try to play nice, the more comfortable I am with any power I've earned."

ACV, short for curriculum vitae, is a formal and complete documentation of your academic and professional accomplishments. Chances are you have a résumé or bio, but not a CV.

Although I haven't used my curriculum vitae often, I found the process of writing it to be one of the most exciting, self-affirming tasks I've ever done in my professional life. As I look at my CV, I get an overwhelming sense of personal pride as well as a realization that I really have done a lot in my career. Right on!

A CV should contain at least some of the following sections:

- Employment history
- Boards and organizational affiliations
- Educational background
- Awards and recognition
- Publishing and media
- Special interests and additional information

Take a look at some actual CVs online at:

Toni Morrison
> www.nobel.se/literature/laureates/1993/morrison-cv.html

Dr. Elaine Martin
> bama.ua.edu/~emartin/vitae/

Alice Sowaal
> www.ags.uci.edu/~sowaal/curriculum_vitae.htm

Bonnie Zimmerman
> www-rohan.sdsu.edu/~bzimmerm/cv.html

Wendy L. McGoodwin
www.vgard.net/pages/wlm_cv.html

Think of your CV as a high-powered résumé where tooting your own horn is not only acceptable, it is expected. Keep this document readily available on your computer so you can add to it as you accomplish something new. Mark a day on your calendar each month for the rest of the year to revisit your accomplishments and update your CV.

From now on, when people ask for either your biography or résumé, offer to attach your CV as well. Be proud of your accomplishments, and let them be known!

PERSONAL PROJECT #2:

MAKE YOUR OWN MEDIA KIT

Unless you deal regularly with the press, chances are you don't have your own Media Kit. But why shouldn't you? No matter who you are or what you do, a Media Kit is a great way to promote yourself to others, not just the press.

For those of you with a publicity department, have you seen your Media Kit lately? You may want to carefully review what is being sent out on your behalf. Is it current? Is it compelling? Does it really do you justice?

Keep in mind that this Media Kit is for YOU, not your company.

For those of you without a Media Kit or those who want to improve their Kit, you will need the following supplies:

- A box of nice folders with pockets, usually 25 to a box. Choose a color that is compatible with your logo. You can buy folders that are glossy, recycled, transparent—choose the look that suits your image.

- A ream of good paper. Bright white and at least 20 lb. weight is a good place to start; check fine paper stores if you are looking for something different. Don't go too crazy with the paper, however, as you want the text to be clear and legible.
- Twenty-five black and white matte or glossy photographs of you. The photos should be in the form of a professional headshot—not a casual snapshot or full-body shot—something newspapers can easily print. The ideal and standard dimension for media kit photographs are 8 x 10.
- Box of Avery Labels. You can choose the size and shape of the labels, however, three inches by four inches is a nice rectangular space where you can print your company logo or name in a clean font. Stick these on the front of each folder, in the center, toward the top. If you already have stickers with your company logo, use them instead.
- Twenty-five business cards. Most pocket folders have slots for business cards. Or you can attach your card to the folder in a variety of ways, including stylish paper clips (I've seen gold ones shaped in a spiral that look great) or non-permanent glue (the kind that makes a surface tacky but doesn't stick or rip the paper).

What are the key elements of a media kit? You should try to include at least a biography, CV, press releases, media clips, positive testimonials from other people about you, or articles you've written.

Assemble a box of Media Kits for yourself, then identify 25 people you think might be interested in you—potential clients, the media, or even friends and family. Attach a very brief cover letter to the front of the kit explaining what it is all about.

If you have a PR person, you can get them to do this for you, but regardless, you should take charge of the way you are presented to and perceived by the outside world.

Your media kit is one of your tools to build your own personal brand and share your accomplishments with others.

PERSONAL PROJECT #3:

SPEAK IN PUBLIC

Those of us who speak in public take the process for granted. Whether we've grown accustomed to public speaking over time or been comfortable speaking in front of an audience from Day One, the act of standing in front of others, opening our mouths, and letting our voice out is empowering.

If you have never spoken in front of an audience, find an opportunity to do so. You don't have to go out and book a speaking engagement. An easy way to get a chance to speak publicly, although more informally, is at business networking events. Many of these events allow members a chance to stand up and either introduce themselves or go to a microphone and ask questions.

Investigate networking meetings in your area, particularly ones you have never attended before, and find out which ones allow attendees to speak to the group in some format. Also, choose a meeting where at least 50 people attend each month. Then prepare what you want to say about yourself beforehand.

If attendees are introducing themselves, make sure you prepare—in writing—your own brief intro, with the emphasis on brief. Include your:

- Name
- Title

• Company name or what you do. Try to condense this into one sentence that easily explains what you do to any layperson. Do not use jargon.

When I ran Cybergrrl, I would say:

My name is Aliza Sherman. I'm president of Cybergrrl, Inc., an Internet media company that publishes three sites for women and consults major corporations and nonprofit organizations on reaching women online, and founder of Webgrrls International, a global Internet networking group for women with over 100 chapters around the world.

Whew! A bit of a mouthful, but after saying it over and over again, I finally didn't need to jot notes down for myself.

Next, follow everyone else's lead as to what else you should say. Maybe they say why they are attending the meeting or what they are looking for in terms of help, resources, or information. Again, keep your responses to one sentence.

If you are at a panel discussion or lecture and attendees are allowed to ask questions at the end, prepare your question as you are listening to what is being said. Even if you do not have an actual question, formulate a universally appealing one that you can direct to one or all of the panelists. Why? Because you want to get in front of the microphone and let everyone know who you are.

Definitely jot down what you are going to say as the panel is in session because by the time it is your turn at the microphone, your adrenaline will be surging, your heart will be pounding, and your mouth will go dry.

If you are really interested in public speaking, national organizations such as Toastmasters and the National Speakers Association have local chapters, meetings, and resources for aspiring and professional speakers.

Speaking in front of others takes practice, but after you do it once or twice, you'll find yourself getting more and more bold. Go for it!

POWERTOOL 9 CHECKLIST

Be Comfortable with Power

- *Never apologize for being powerful.*
- *Don't be afraid to brag about your accomplishments. Toot your own horn!*
- *Recognize your powers as a woman in business and use them to your advantage.*
- *If you haven't already, try speaking in public. Find your voice and let it be heard.*

NUGGETS

BOOKS ON PUBLIC SPEAKING

In the Spotlight: Overcome Your Fear of Public Speaking and Performing, Janet E. Esposito, Strong Books, 2000

101 Secrets of Highly Effective Speakers: Controlling Fear, Commanding Attention, Caryl Rae Krannich, Impact Publications, 1998

101 Ways to Captivate a Business Audience, Sue Gaulke, AMACOM, 1996

7 Steps to Fearless Speaking, Lilyan Wilder, John Wiley & Sons, 1999

WEB SITES FOR PUBLIC SPEAKERS

Toastmasters
   www.toastmasters.org
National Speakers Association
   www.nsaspeaker.org
Public Speaking Resources
   www.college.hmco.com/communications/public/index.htm

Chapter 10

GIVE BACK

When You've Got It, Spread It Around

*"A cup that is already full cannot have more added to it.
In order to receive the further good to which we are entitled,
we must give of that which we have."*

—**Margaret Becker**

PATRICIA "TRISH" PATTERSON IS CEO OF CONSULTING SOFTWARE and Services (DCSS) and has a history of creating "social enterprise programs"—social programs implemented as part of her business—that benefit more than just her company's bottom line. Trish believes technology can be harnessed for a greater good and a person's physical limitations should not hold them back. Technology is a work-force equalizer and that notion was the catalyst for Trish founding DCSS Ability (DCSSA), a company jointly owned by the Cerebral Palsy Research Foundation (CPRF) and DCSS, Trish's consulting company.

At DCSSA, they not only train the physically handicapped for careers in high-tech, but also employ them. Plus, they fill the unmet need for high-tech workers.

Explains Trish, "By forming DCSSA, I feel that I am not offering a hand-out, but a helping hand. I truly believe that the blessings given to you should be passed on to others. I am proud to say that I am helping those with disabilities gain the skills they need to enter the work force and contribute effectively."

Finding ways to create a company or part of your company that "does good" is often the most fulfilling way to do business. The adage "Doing Well by Doing Good" is something we should all live and work by.

SHE READS

Recommended by Trish Patterson, founder and CEO of Digital Consulting and Software Ability (DCSSA):

Zapp!—The Lightning of Empowerment by William C. Byham, Ph.D. with Jeff Cox
"[The author suggests that if you] empower and motivate your employees to achieve their potential they will build an organization better than you can conceive."

Building Leaders: How Successful Companies Develop the Next Generation by Jay Alden Conger and Beth Benjamin

"[This book shows that] next to profits, having a succession plan for the roles in your company and preparing multiple employees to be ready to step into those roles is the best thing you can do for your employees and the organization."

Plan to Win by Bill Glass
"[Glass says to] only do those tasks that align with your goals."

The New Strategic Selling by Stephen E. Heiman and Diane Sanchez with Tad Tuleja

---

> "[This book says] you should understand that there are multiple buyers in every account and be able to identify who they are: the coach, end-user, technical, and economic buyer."
>
> *The Go-Getter: A Story That Tells You How to Be One* by Peter B. Kyne
>
> "[Kyne's advice is] do not let obstacles get in your way; find a way to be successful!"

THE ART OF GIVING

There are two parts to the idea of giving back that are essential for you to keep in mind. When you hear the words "give back," do you automatically think of giving something back to your community or giving to charity?

There is another equally important aspect of "giving back"—the act of giving back to yourself. Even in business, whether out of sheer focus or neglect, women tend to be selfless or to ignore themselves until both they and their business suffer. Don't let that happen to you!

> ### E-QUOTE: HEATHER O'NEIL, COFOUNDER, ETRAVELPLAN.COM
>
> *"I try to start each day with one or two things I want to accomplish, and I make sure I do them before I leave. That way, I at least get those things done with all the other meetings, phone calls, and e-mails I get.*

"I have a number of to-do lists, for me and those I work with. That way I can keep track of what is going on. I also try to take short classes on different parts of the industry to learn new skills and meet new people.

"In addition, I always have a vacation planned so I have some personal time to look forward to. Thailand is in a few weeks, and I'm thinking about Europe for 2001."

YOUR COMMUNITY, YOUR WORLD

Now that you've had a moment to think about giving to yourself, we can consider the "giving to others" category. Imagine having a business where you are totally fulfilled, challenged, stimulated, and able to do good things that have a positive effect on the world. Laura Scher helped to create that kind of business and work for herself.

Laura Scher is a cofounder of Working Assets, a long-distance, credit card, and online services company that is arguably the top corporate role model of donation-linked products.

The Working Assets business model is built around giving back to the community by donating a portion of the company's revenue to progressive nonprofit groups each year. The company is dedicated to "building a world that is more just, humane, and environmentally sustainable." Over the last 15 years, Working Assets has donated more than $25 million to nonprofit organizations. Laura's aim is to grow the company so it can give $10 million in donations each year.

Before cofounding Working Assets, Laura was in business school and looking for a career that combined her interest in social change with business. She and others founded Working Assets to offer people a way to spend in a socially responsible fashion. They wanted everyday activities, like talking on the phone or buying a book, to become acts of social change.

Laura believes that none of us need to "leave our values at the door when we go to work." Working Assets is a company that combines personal values and goals with good business because people should not have to compromise their values at their workplace.

In terms of what you can do to incorporate social responsibility into your work and business, Laura says the process can be as easy as instituting a recycling program or adopting a high school class or donating toiletries you collect on business trips to homeless shelters.

Says Laura, "If you care about social justice, the environment, and peace, you can make your workplace an effective place for social change."

If you ask Gabrielle Melchionda about the underlying philosophy of her company Mad Gab's, producers of natural lip and body balms, she'll point you to her company's web site and mission. Part of the mission statement reads: "To create jobs for people in my community (myself included), and for local shelters who employ folks with a variety of emotional and physical challenges."

True to her mission, Mad Gab's employs developmentally and physically challenged adults to label and shrink-wrap their products. Her company takes good care of their employees, offering flextime, job sharing, health insurance, and profit-sharing. In the works are pension plans and paid volunteer time.

With a clear vision for building a responsible company, something that is also stated in her company mission ("To participate in revolutionizing capitalism with honesty, integrity, and sound business practices."), Gabrielle seems to have found an approach that works well for business.

So how does Gabrielle ensure that Mad Gab's mission always guides what her company does? She meets periodically with her team to discuss what they are doing. This year will be the first that Mad Gab's has the financial means to put their money where their mission is. They are planning to give almost 9 percent of their pre-tax profits to local organizations the team has selected, including Maine Women and Girls Foundation, Community Partners (the organization that provides the workers who handle Mad Gab's packaging), and an environmental group.

Says Gabrielle, "We are succeeding because we love what we do, we have a vision in common, and we are having fun at work. It feels right, we do good things, make great products and the rest just seems to happen. We call it the magic of Mad Gab's." Or the magic of giving back.

Paula Jagemann's firm, EC12, is a strong supporter of nonprofit organizations. As a private citizen, Paula also gives generously to two national organizations to which she consistently donates and she actively supports several local organizations.

Advocates for the Homeless in Frederick, Maryland, is one organization that Paula supports. They not only shelter homeless women and their children, but also empower their participants by placing them in a four-year program of education and job training so they will become functioning, self-sufficient individuals. Within the past year, Paula's firm has given this group more than they had received in total the two years prior. Paula has also contributed personally to the group.

Another organization Paula supports is Frisky's Wildlife and Primate Sanctuary in Woodsboro, Maryland, run by Colleen, a Native

American. Paula heard of Colleen after her ten-year-old nephew took a chick that had been born with a deformed leg to Colleen's sanctuary at the suggestion of the Humane Society. Colleen made a wooden leg for the chick and Paula began receiving newsletters from the sanctuary.

Through the newsletter, Paula learned about a specific fund-raising campaign to build a new monkey house for the larger primates at the sanctuary. The goal was to raise $10,000, and over the following weeks and months, Colleen sold her van and had garage sales to raise the money. Paula couldn't believe that after months of campaigning and selling off her own property, Colleen could only raise $2000.

Paula called Colleen that morning and said she was going to match any donation for the monkey house up to $5,000. The campaign was an overwhelming success, and last year Colleen built The Jagemann Monkey House. Few things have meant more to Paula and her family than being able to provide something for people—or animals—in need.

From a business standpoint, Paula's company, ECI2, devotes its primary philanthropic efforts to the Cystic Fibrosis Foundation (CFF). Paula first became involved with the CFF in 1998 when the disease struck close to home, affecting two family members. ECI2 has sponsored several teams to participate in the CFF's annual Cystic Fibrosis Challenge.

As a businesswoman, Paula feels that corporate giving opportunities create brand awareness, can help to generate sales, and offer the company tax deductions. Most importantly, she also believes the act of giving will create a more positive corporate culture as diverse employees rally around a cause and form bonds.

Paula does have a few words of warning before you set out to save the world, such as be careful not to wander into controversial territory with any charity you choose to support on a corporate level.

Keep in mind the varied lives and beliefs of your employees and choose an organization that is universally appealing, such as one that fights hunger or homelessness, or supports children or animals. Other neutral causes can be sponsoring families at the holidays, toy drives, and blood drives.

According to Paula, "Giving isn't just a 'nice' thing to do. It's the 'right' thing to do. The more common giving becomes within the boundaries of corporate America, the healthier we are as a society."

When successful women such as Laura, Gabrielle, and Paula talk about the importance of giving back, it is easy to see that they are gaining both personally and professionally from doing so. Their stories prove it is possible to build a company around a foundation of giving and still have financial success. You can start giving in small ways and grow as your company grows. The act of giving will create growth in ways you may have never expected.

PERSONAL PROJECT #1:
CHOOSE A CAUSE

There are many excuses not to give to charities. Let's look at these excuses individually.

Excuse #1: I can't figure out what organization I should give to. What do you believe in? What do you feel strongly about? Identifying a cause that matches your values and interests is a way to strengthen your own identity. Doing a search online for "nonprofit organizations" will lead to pages and pages of possibilities. Narrowing your search by looking for "nonprofit, animals" or "nonprofit, girls" or "nonprofit, environment, New Jersey" can help you pinpoint a specific organization that may strike a chord with you.

Excuse #2: I have no money. One could argue that you bought this book for yourself so chances are you have a few dollars to spare for someone else. You do not have to be rich to give. Even $5 or $10 each month to a local charity adds up to $60 or $120 per year. If 100 businesswomen did the same thing, that organization could expect between $6,000 and $12,000 that year. For small organizations, that could actually be half of their entire annual income or half the annual salary for a paid staff member.

Excuse #3: I have no time. None of us feel we have time to spare, but even one hour each month could mean more to a local organization or person in need than you can ever imagine. Go online to a site like VolunteerMatch.com and there you can find organizations that match not only your interests but the parameters of the commitment you are willing to make. When I did a search on the site, I even found an organization that was looking for people with friendly dogs to bring to a local nursing home for a few hours a month. If your pet can contribute their time to a good cause, so can you.

Excuse #4: How do I know my money is doing any good or is being used for what they claim? If you are concerned whether or not your money is actually being used for what an organization claims, make sure you work with nationally or locally known groups. Ask around before you open your checkbook. You can see the impact of your money if you contribute in the following ways:

- Work with a small, local group where you can visit their site and see your money at work.
- Specify when you give your money exactly what you want it to go to and ask to be able to check back to see the results of your contribution. For example, let them know you are making a $3,000 contribution to go toward purchasing a computer and

printer for their office. Then schedule a visit to their office within the next month to see the computer being used.

- Give in-kind donations. If you have an old computer, give it to a local charity and schedule time to show them how to hook up and operate it. You'll see your contribution in action.

The cause or causes you choose to support tell others something about you. Choose your cause wisely and don't be afraid to let others know that you are contributing. Some people want to remain anonymous in their giving. However, if you are public about it, you will influence others to contribute as well.

PERSONAL PROJECT #2:

SPRING CLEAN FOR CHARITY

Have you looked in your closet lately? When was the last time you wore that suit? Or those sensible pumps? Or that scarf? Even if it isn't spring, put aside a few hours this weekend to go through all of your business clothes and pull out anything you haven't worn in the last year.

Next, get in touch with Dress for Success and find out how you can donate your suits and professional-looking accessories to help other women. Dress for Success is a nonprofit organization that helps low-income women make transitions into the work force. Each Dress for Success client receives one suit when she has an interview and a second suit when she gets the job.

Women are referred to Dress for Success by other nonprofit member organizations, including homeless shelters, domestic violence shelters, job training programs, and English as a second language programs.

If there is not a Dress for Success affiliate nearby, you may want to help the organization bring its program to your community by contacting the national office (www.dressforsuccess.org).

E-QUOTE: NANCY LUBLIN,

FOUNDER, DRESS FOR SUCCESS

NANCY: It is really hard to work, raise a family, have time for yourself, and do charity. I hope women don't feel guilty about the fact that they are often too busy to get personally involved. We're the charity for those women. They can pull three suits from their closet and send them or drop them off and help three women interview for jobs looking and feeling terrific. The idea behind Dress for Success is that the gift is from one woman to another.

    Cleaning out your closet is cathartic. I just did it last weekend myself, and I gave away a couple of expensive numbers that I never thought I would part with. But they did no good hanging in the back of my closet. I know I just gave power suits to two women. That made me feel good and my closet looks fab. Open up that closet door and start giving!

POWERTOOL 10 CHECKLIST

Give Back

- *Remember the importance of giving to yourself. You'll then have more to give to others.*
- *When giving on a personal level, don't be afraid to start small or stay local. Every little bit counts, anywhere it is given.*

- *For business, choose charities or causes that are more universal and less controversial in order to involve all of your employees.*
- *If you have it, you can now give it away. Know what is essential for you to keep and what can be donated to someone in need.*

NUGGETS

BOOKS ABOUT GIVING

Inspired Philanthropy, Tracy Gary et. al., Chardon Press, 1998

Don't Just Give It Away: How to Make the Most of Your Charitable Giving, Renata J. Rafferty and Paul Newman, Chandler House Press, 1999

Common Interest, Common Good: Creating Value Through Business and Social Sector Partnerships, Shirley Sagawa et. al., Harvard Business School Press, 1999

WEB SITES FOR ONLINE GIVING

GreaterGood.com
    www.greatergood.com
iGive.com
    www.igive.com
iReachOut.com
    www.ireachout.com/
Shop for Change
    www.shopforchange.com
VolunteerMatch.com
    www.volunteermatch.com

Chapter 11

IT STARTS WITH YOU

Honor Your True Self and the Rest Will Follow

"If you think you can, you can.
And if you think you can't, you're right."

—**Mary Kay Ash**

YOU CAN LOOK AT THE WORLD IN TWO DIFFERENT WAYS: FILLED WITH obstacles or rich with challenges. You either choose the glass-half-empty or glass-half-full approach. But, bottom line, it all starts with you and how well you know and believe in yourself. Using the PowerTools is one way to learn more about yourself and acquire inner skills to face challenges, overcome obstacles, and reach your goals.

Being aware of the global impact of your life and work is essential to realizing your fullest potential. What you do each day matters. What you say and how you act and react has a profound effect on more than just your business. Understanding how everything you do is connected and how everything you are should be connected, too, is the first step to fulfilling your life's potential.

The PowerTools are meant to help you look closely at your life, how you spend your time and energy, and the direction in which you are going. Always return to what you feel in your heart and gut first, then create the path using your head. If you are feeling unfulfilled, your path needs adjustment. If you are feeling fulfilled, do more of whatever you did to get there!

The PowerTools should help you not only live in the best way you can but also work and build your business in the best way. Since our work and lives are so interconnected, living well can help us work well and vice versa.

Mastering the PowerTools takes practice, dedication, and a strong belief that you are worth it. If you didn't have that belief when you first opened this book, I hope you have it now, or at least the seed of it. After reading the stories of all of the women in the book, I hope you know you are not alone.

Are you going to live to work? Or are you going to work to live? You are ultimately the only one who can decide how you will live your life. My advice?

Live your life to its fullest and find your joy.

And don't forget to cut out the PowerTools and post them somewhere to remind you of your power. Use the PowerTools. Make them work for you. Create the life and work that you want, one step at a time.

MY POWERTOOLS

1. Share Your Stories
2. Take Charge of Change
3. Never Stop Learning
4. Overcome Crisis
5. Tackle Technology
6. Mold Your Mission
7. Be a Mentor
8. Nurture Your Network
9. Wield Your Power
10. Give Back

APPENDIX

CHAPTER 1

JENNIFER C. KING, FOUNDER AND DIRECTOR, BIOSPACE.COM, INC.
www.biospace.com
BioSpace.com is an e-solutions provider and the leading Internet hub-site for the life sciences industry.
Founded 1985.

JENAI LANE, PRINCIPAL, ZEAL CO.
www.zealco.com
Zeal Co. is a business consulting firm specializing in branding, product development, and public relations.
Founded 2000.

CHAPTER 2

HEATHER DUKE, PRESIDENT, PROFOUNDIA
www.Profoundia.com
Profoundia is a retailer and wholesaler of body adornment products, including Bindi bodydots, crystal tattoos, henna, and fashion jewelry from India.
Founded 1999.

BRENDA K. STIER, PRESIDENT, MARKETING WORKS, INC.
www.marketing-works.net
Marketing Works is a full-service public relations firm, specializing in business-to-business marketing.
Founded 1995.

RACHEL ALEXANDER, DIRECTOR, ALEXANDERS ADVERTISING LTD.
www.alexanders.co.nz
A direct marketing and advertising agency that works with clients to find and attract new customers while retaining and growing the existing customer base.
Founded 1996.

MARY AZZARTO, CEO, PLUMB DESIGN, INC.
www.plumbdesign.com
Plumb Design, Inc., designs and develops software, Web applications, and communication platforms.
Founded 1997.

KATHERINE WELDON, CEO, eTIME SOLUTIONS, INC.
www.etimesolutions.com
eTime Solutions is an Internet applications development and intregration company.
Founded 1999.

CHAPTER 3

SHARON GOLDMACHER, PRESIDENT, COMMUNICATIONS 21, INC.
www.c21pr.com
communications 21 is a marketing public relations firm providing media relations, special event planning/implementation, and multimedia expertise, including web site development.
Founded 1992.

CHRISTINE O'BRIEN, OWNER, DESIGNWRITE PRESENTATIONS
www.deswrite.com
DesignWrite Presentations provides graphic design and PR writing

services for small businesses who need to present themselves in print or on the Web.
Founded 1997.

PAULINE LALLY, PRESIDENT, PIPING SYSTEMS, INC.
www.piping-systems-inc.com
Piping Systems, Inc. is an open shop mechanical contractor serving the commercial, industrial, and institutional industries with the capability to design/build, install, and/or prefabricate assemblies for any piping application.
Founded 1971.

BETH LEWIS, PRESIDENT, COMPUTER COACH, INC.
www.computercoach.com
Computer Coach is a computer & technical school for adults. It also develops, hosts, and markets web sites for small- to mid-sized businesses and nonprofit organizations.
Founded 1992.

SHERRY HARSCH-PORTER, PRESIDENT, PORTER BAY GROUP
www.porterbay.com
The Porter Bay Group is an international human resources consulting firm devoted to maximizing profits through Human Capital.
Founded 2000.

TAMARA REMEDIOS, PRESIDENT/OWNER, XPLORE COMMUNCIATIONS
www.getouttoday.com/xplore
Xplore Communications is a marketing agency that produces a college publication, *Get Out Today*, and provides marketing consultation to small businesses.
Founded 1999.

CHRISTINE HARMEL, CEO, THE INTERACTIVE RESOURCE
www.interactiveresource.com
The Interactive Resource is a matchmaker of interactive services that helps clients find the best Web design company and other resources for their projects.
Founded 1998.

CARYN CAMERON, OWNER, PRAXIS CONSULTING
web site pending
Praxis Consulting offers Web design, software assistance, and tutoring on Macs and PCs.
Founded 1987.

CARMEN MATTHEWS, OWNER, DIRECTOR, AND AUTONOMOUS FEM COACH, SERENE SAMURAI
www.femcourage.com
Serene Samurai provides Autonomous Fem Coach Mother/Daughter Coaching, Individualized Anger Management, and Organizational Behavior Coaching designed to promote healthy self-esteem.
Founded 1999.

NANCY GING, OWNER, TURTLE ISLAND WEB DESIGN
turtle.camano.net
Turtle Island Web Design offers web site design and development and Web design training services.
Founded 1995.

KIM FISHER, CEO, AUDIOBASKET
audiobasket.com
San Francisco-based AudioBasket has developed an exclusive technology that allows keyword personalization of audio news and

information on the Web and beyond.
Founded 1999.

LIZ COBB, FOUNDER AND EXECUTIVE VICE PRESIDENT INCENTIVE SYSTEMS
www.incentivesystems.com
Incentive Systems develops enterprise incentive management (EIM) software applications that enable companies to implement effective incentive compensation plans to achieve corporate goals across the extended enterprise.
Founded 1997.

CHAPTER 4

MARY SCHANZER, OWNER, PARTY PERSONNEL, LLC
Party Personnel provides banquet servers and bartenders to hotels, country clubs, and caterers on a temporary, as-needed basis.
Founded 1993.

LORRAINE AHO, FOUNDER, SACREDHOME.COM
www.sacredhome.com
SacredHome.com offers authentic spiritual arts and crafts.
Founded 1999.

SUZI BERMAN, PRESIDENT/CREATIVE DIRECTOR, D MEDIA, INC.
www.dmedia-inc.com
D Media, Inc., is a graphic design studio providing creative solutions for brochures, logos, annual reports, corporate identity, newsletters, direct mail, and web site design and development.
Founded 1995.

HEIDI VAN ARNEM, FOUNDER AND CEO, iCAN.COM
www.ican.com
ICan is the leading online community for people with disabilities.
Founded 1998.

MICHELLE LEMMONS-POSCENTE, PRESIDENT, INTERNATIONAL SPEAKERS
BUREAU
www.InternationalSpeakers.com
ISB places speakers and entertainment internationally for top Fortune
500 companies.
Founded 1993.

JULIE COOK DOWNING, FOUNDER AND PRESIDENT, CAREGIVER'S COM-
FORT™ CREATIONS, LLC
www.caregiverscomfort.com
Caregiver's Comfort™ Creations, LLC, produces motivational tools
and provides resources and seminars for the growing population of
caregivers.
Incorporated 2000.

PATSY BRUCE, PRESIDENT AND CEO, PAB CORPORATION
PAB Corporation is a holding company for several entrepreneurial
ventures, including Events Unlimited and Patsy Bruce Productions.
Founded 1984.

CYNTHIA HARRIS, PRESIDENT, STRATEGY ASSOCIATES, INC.
www.strategyassociates.com
Strategy Associates, Inc., develops and launches global and domestic
public relations campaigns for high-technology companies.
Founded 1990.

CHAPTER 5

KATHY LONG, HEAD HONCHO, KAT AND MOUSE WEB DESIGN
www.katandmouse.com
Kat and Mouse designs and develops web sites—from the simple billboard site to ones with full e-commerce and database capabilities.
Founded 1997.

HEIDI ALLEN, FOUNDER AND PRESIDENT, KNOWLEDGE HOUND, LLC
www.knowledgehound.com
Knowledge Hound is a Web directory of how-tos for thousands of
topics.
Founded 1997.

BRENDA KAHN, PRESIDENT, WOMANROCK
www.womanrock.com
The mission of WOMANROCK is to support emerging voices in
women's music, promoting artists through its online magazine and
providing a distribution network for online sales of independent
records.
Founded 1999.

JANET R. YOUNG, PRESIDENT, JRY DEVELOPMENT CORP.
www.jrydevelopment.com
JRY Development provides web site development and networking/
inter-office connectivity solutions for individuals and small- to medium-
sized businesses.
Founded 1998.

MICHELLE LAWLOR, FOUNDER AND CEO, EKINDNESS.COM
www.ekindness.com
eKindness.com is a self-help/self-esteem company that provides

products and information that help women lead more productive lives. *Founded 1999.*

KRISTINE HANNA, CEO AND COFOUNDER, GIRLGEEKS
www.girlgeeks.com
A career success site for women in IT.
Founded 1998.

HELEN DRISCOLL, FOUNDER AND DIRECTOR, FINE PAPER COMPANY/ INVITESITE.COM
www.invitesite.com
Fine Paper Company designs and fabricates signature environmental and fine papers for personal and business use. InviteSite.com provides specialty printing software and letterpress printing.
Founded 1995.

RANDY EPSTEIN, PRESIDENT, MY RED SHOES, LLC
www.myredshoesllc.com
Personal advisors for people interested in creating their own financial futures.
Founded 2000.

PHYLLIS DEL PICO, FOUNDER/DIRECTOR, RECRUITERSONCALL.COM
RecruitersOnCall.com provides talent to companies who need technical staffing and career development services to individuals who desire a change.
Founded 1999.

LORRAINE M. PASQUALI, FOUNDER AND PRESIDENT, IMAGINESTATION
www.imaginestation.net
Imaginestation is a Web portal for the creative community that provides the resources necessary for artists of all types to communicate

with a global audience as well as each other.
Founded 2000.

PAULA QUENEMOEN, EXECUTIVE VICE PRESIDENT, JAGGED EDGE MOUNTAIN GEAR
www.jaggededge.com
Jagged Edge Mountain Gear is a manufacturer of technical outerwear and rugged mountain wear with divisions and distribution in wholesale, retail stores, e-commerce, and mail order.
Founded 1991.

CHAPTER 6

ANDREA KAY, AUTHOR, SYNDICATED COLUMNIST, CAREER CONSULTANT, ART OF SELF DIRECTION
www.andreakay.com
Andrea works one-on-one with people in all professions on career issues and writes books and a weekly syndicated newspaper column about careers and the workplace.
Founded 1990.

CAREY EARLE, PRESIDENT, HARVEST CONSULTING GROUP
www.harvestconsult.com
Harvest Consulting Group is a marketing and branding firm that works with companies to build or evolve their brand position in the minds and hearts of customers, employees, and everyone their business touches.
Founded 1999.

GEETHA P. RAJAN, PRINCIPAL AND MANAGING DIRECTOR, ITEC RESOURCES
www.itecresources.com
Itec Resources is a technical search firm that specializes in assisting

companies locate and hire quality Information Technology talent. *Founded 1999.*

JOY RADLE, PRESIDENT AND FOUNDER, ALL MARCOM, LLC
www.allmarcom.com
All MarCom, LLC, is an independent marketing communications firm that specializes in integrating traditional and online marketing communications with Web-enabled sales processes.
Founded 1993.

ORIT, PRESIDENT AND CEO, THE O GROUP
www.ogroup.net
The O Group is a full-service marketing communications firm, with three specialized divisions: O Interactive (Web design and development), O Design (print), and Oz Promotions (premiums/promotions).
Founded 1986.

JANICE CAILLET, CHIEF CATALYST, COACHING CIRCLES, A SERVICE OF PARTNERS IN LIFE, INC.
www.coachingcircles.com
A full service coaching company dedicated to your professional and personal growth.
Founded 1999.

JILL HARRISON, PRESIDENT AND FOUNDER, ISOLE DEVELOPMENT
www.isole.com
Isole designs and sells handmade Italian leather luggage via catalog, on the Web, and through selected retail stores.
Founded 1997.

DONNA CRAFTON, COFOUNDER AND VICE PRESIDENT, PUBLIC RELATIONS, LH3, INC.
www.lh3.com
LH3 is an interactive PR and marketing firm focused on providing innovative and strategic public relations and marketing services to clients to build awareness, reputation, and bottom-line profitability.
Founded 2000.

DEBBIE TOMPKINS, FOUNDER AND PRESIDENT, TOMPKINS BENEFIT GROUP
www.tompkinsbenefit.com
Tompkins Benefit Group provides strategies, implementation, and ongoing management of plans to help employers attract and retain quality employees through the use of employee benefits.
Founded 1995.

CAROLINE CARMAGNOL, CEO, ALIZE PUBLIC RELATIONS
Alize PR provides strategic marketing and public relations services to European hi-tech start-up companies wishing to expand their business into the United States.
Founded 1998.

CHAPTER 7

LISA KRUSS, PRESIDENT AND CEO, INTERNET PRESENCE CONSULTING, INC.
www.ipcinc.net
IPC develops exceptionally designed Web presences that are creative, interactive, easy to navigate, and provide for future scalability.
Founded 1996.

Jennifer Floren, President and CEO, experience.com, Inc.
www.experience.com
experience.com is the leader in the college student and alumni "e-cruiting" market, working to help match top talent with top employers through online and on-campus recruiting services and *experience* magazine.
Founded 1996.

Robin Lutchansky, President, Lutchansky Communications
www.LComm.com
A high-tech public relations agency.
Founded 1996.

Gwen McIvor, President, BridgeLight Group
BridgeLight provides e-business training and consulting for nontech businesses as well as strategic marketing planning for technology companies.
Founded 1998.

Debbie Bernard, President, Bernard Marketing Associates
A firm which provides marketing and management consulting to builders, developers, banking, and other real estate-related clients in the Western United States.
Founded 1991.

CHAPTER 8

Sally Meecham, Founder and CEO, Traveldonkey Limited
www.traveldonkey.com
The global travel review site that is written by you, for you.
Founded 2000.

LUCY ROSEN, PRESIDENT, THE BUSINESS DEVELOPMENT GROUP
www.businessdevelopmentgroup.com
A marketing, public relations, and business development firm that helps companies grow.
Founded 1985.

CANDY MIRRER, PRESIDENT AND FOUNDER, MIRRERSEARCH.COM
www.mirrersearch.com
MirrerSearch.com recruits talented individuals to build companies and leaders in the New Economy and provides an array of business consulting services.
Founded 1999.

KATHLEEN ZEMAITIS, PRESIDENT AND FOUNDER, ZINE COMMUNICATIONS
A public relations firm which provides strategic planning, development, and execution of public relations communications programs.
Founded 1997.

CHAPTER 9

STEPHANIE SPENCE, PUBLISHER, SPENCE PUBLISHING
www.healthymag.com
Custom publishing company that creates and publishes signature magazines, *Pennsylvania Health & Fitness* magazine and *Pittsburgh NOW*.
Founded 1994.

ALEXANDRIA K. BROWN, FOUNDER AND PRESIDENT, AKB & ASSOCIATES
www.akbwriting.com
A copywriting/editing firm specializing in writing for high-end marketing communications.
Founded 1998.

ALISON BERKE MORANO, PRESIDENT, BWORKS.COM, INC.
www.bworks.com
bworks.com specializes in Web design, Internet marketing, and database consulting.
Founded 1995.

KIMBERLY L. McCALL, PRESIDENT, McCALL MEDIA AND MARKETING, INC.
www.MarketingAngel.com
McCall Media & Marketing, Inc., is a business communications company.
Founded 1997.

CHAPTER 10

PATRICIA "TRISH" PATTERSON, CEO, CONSULTING SOFTWARE & SERVICES (DCSS)
www.dcss.com
DCSS offers full-service consulting and technology strategizing.
Founded 1990.

HEATHER O'NEIL, COFOUNDER, ETRAVELPLAN.COM
www.etravelplan.com
eTravelplan.com provides current, qualifed destination information that can be used to create free custom travel guides.
Founded 1999.

LAURA SCHER, COFOUNDER, CHAIR, AND CEO, WORKING ASSETS
www.workingassets.com
Working Assets is a long-distance, credit card, and online services company that helps citizens speak out on issues of critical public concern

through online activism and donates a portion of revenues to progressive nonprofit groups each year.
Founded 1985.

GABRIELLE MELCHIONDA, PRESIDENT, MAD GAB'S, INC.
www.madgabs.com
Manufacturers of all-natural lip and body balms.
Founded 1991.

PAULA JAGEMANN, FOUNDER, PRESIDENT, AND CEO, ECOMMERCE INDUSTRIES, INC. (ECI2)
www.eci2.com
eCommerce Industries, Inc. (ECI2), is the leading provider of information technology solutions to the office products and other reseller-based industries.
Founded 1998.

NANCY LUBLIN, FOUNDER, DRESS FOR SUCCESS
www.dressforsuccess.org
A nonprofit organization that helps low-income women make transitions into the workforce.
Founded 1996.

RESOURCES

BOOKS OF WOMEN'S STORIES

American Women's Autobiography: Fea(s)ts of Memory, Margo Culley, ed., Wisconsin Press, 1992

In Her Own Words: Women's Memoirs from Australia, New Zealand, Canada and the United States, Jill Ker Conway, ed., Vintage Books, April 1999

A Sounding of Women: Autobiographies from Unexpected Places. Martha C. Ward, ed., Allyn and Bacon, May 1997

Writing Women's Lives: An Anthology of Autobiographical Narratives by 20th Century American Women Writers, Susan Cahill, ed., Harper Perennial, April 1994

Written by Herself: Autobiographies of American Women: An Anthology, Jill Ker Conway, ed., Vintage Books, November 1992

Written by Herself: Women's Memoirs from Britain, Africa, Asia, and the United States, Jill Ker Conway, ed., Vintage Books, September 1996

BOOKS ON WRITING YOUR LIFE STORY

Living to Tell the Tale: A Guide to the Writing Memoir, Jane Taylor McDonnell, Penguin USA, March 1998

Writing the Memoir: From Truth to Art, Judith Barrington, Eighth Mountain Press, 1997

Your Life As Story: Discovering the 'New Autobiography' and Writing Memoir As Literature, Tristine Rainer, JP Tarcher, April 1998

WEB SITES ABOUT HERSTORY

We Have Lived Important Lives—List of women's biographies
www.lib.ttu.edu/womens_studies/WOMBIO.htm

American Literature
www.library.wisc.edu/libraries/WomensStudies/core/cramlit.htm

The World Wide Web Virtual Library/Women's History
wwwliisg.nl/~womhist/vlwhalph.html

Women's Studies Resources
duncan.cup.edu/~hartman/wsres1.htm

Women's History
womenshistory.about.com/

Women of Achievement and Herstory
www.undelete.org/woa.html

POWERTOOL 2—BE OPEN TO CHANGE

BOOKS ON FENG SHUI

Clear Your Clutter With Feng Shui, Karen Kingston, Broadway Books, 1999

Feng Shui Goes to the Office: How to Thrive from 9 to 5, Nanilee Wydra, Contemporary Books, 2000

Lillian Too's Easy-to-Use Feng Shui, Lillian Too, Sterling Publications, 1999

Move Your Stuff, Change Your Life: How to Use Feng Shui to Get Love, Money, Respect and Happiness, Karen Rauch Carter; Fireside, 2000

The Western Guide to Feng Shui: Room by Room, Terah Kathryn Collins, Hay House, 1999

WEBSITES ON FENG SHUI

About.com's Chinese Culture
http://chineseculture.about.com/culture/chineseculture/cs/
fengshui

Geomancy.net
www.geomancy.net

SpiritWeb: Feng Shui
www.spiritweb.org/Spirit/feng-shui.html

AllFengShui.com
www.alfengshui.com

POWERTOOL 3—LEARN CONSTANTLY

WOMEN'S SOLO TRAVELS

Another Wilderness: Notes from the new Outdoorswoman, Susan Fox Rogers, ed., Seal Press, 1997

The Corporate Mystic: A Guidebook for Visionaries with Their Feet on the Ground, Gay Hendricks and Kate Ludeman, Dell Publishing Group, 1997

The Female Advantage, Sally Helgesen, Currency/Doubleday, 1995

Gifts of the Wild: A Woman's Book of Adventure, Faith Conlon, et.al., Seal Press, 1998

In Our Wildest Dreams, Joline Godfrey, Harperbusiness, 1993

A Journey of One's Own: Uncommon Advice for the Independent Woman Traveler, Thalia Zapata, Eighth Mountain Press, August 1996

Miles from Nowhere: A Round the World Bicycle Adventure, Barbara Savage, Mountaineers Books, 1985

A Passion for Travel: More True Stories from a Woman's World, Travelers' Tales, Inc., 1999

Princessa Machiavelli, Harriet Rubin, Dell, 1998

Solo: On Her Own Adventure, Susan Fox Rogers, editor, Seal Press, 1996

Tracks, Robyn Davidson, Vintage, 1980

Travelers' Tales: Gutsy Women, Travel Tips and Wisdom for the Road, Marybeth Bond, Travelers' Tales, Inc., 1996

Traveler's Tales: Women in the Wild, Lucy McCauley, ed., Travelers' Tales, Inc., 1998

Women Travel: First-hand Accounts From More Than 60 Countries, Natania Jansz, Miranda Davies, Emma Drew and Lori McDougall, eds., The Rough Guides, 1999

A Woman's World, ed. Mary Beth Bond, Travelers' Tales, Inc., 1995

GENERAL COURSES ONLINE

Element K from Ziff Davis
www.elementk.com

Virtual University
www.vu.org

eCollege
www.ecollege.com

World Wide Learn
www.worldwidelearn.com

BUSINESS COURSES ONLINE

Jones International University
www.jonesinternational.edu

Goergia G.L.O.B.E. (Global Learning Online for Business and Education)
www.georgia-globe.org

Keller Graduate School of Management
www.keller.edu

The Open University
www.open.ac.uk

CHAPTER 4—DON'T WAIT FOR A CRISIS

BOOKS ABOUT CREATIVE WRITING AND JOURNALING

Journaling from the Heart, Eldonna Bouton, Whole Heart Publications, 2000

The New Diary: How to Use a Journal for Self-Guidance and Expanded Creativity, Tristine Rainer, JP Tarcher, 1979

Visual Journaling: Going Deeper Than Words, Barbara Ganim, Susan Fox, Quest Books, 1999

Wild Mind: Living the Writer's Life, Natalie Goldberg, Bantam, 1990

Writing Down the Bones: Freeing the Writer Within, Natalie Goldberg, Shambhala, 1986

A Year in the Life: Journaling for Self Discovery, Sheila Bender, Writers Digest Books, 2000

FEMALE MOTIVATIONAL SPEAKERS

JULIE WHITE
  Professional Impact/Personal Power
  Self Esteem for Women

RITA DAVENPORT
  It's Time for You

LAURA BERMAN FORTGANG
  Take Yourself to the Top

CHERYL RICHARDSON
  Take Time for Your Life
  Life Makeovers

POWERTOOL 5—USE TECHNOLOGY AS YOUR TOOL

BASIC WEB BUILDING BOOKS

Creating Killer Websites, Second Edition, David Siegel, Hayden Books, 1997

HTML for Dummies, Ed. Tittle, IDG Books Worldwide Inc, 1997

HTML: The Definitive Guide, Chuck Musciano, O'Reilly Books, 2000

Teach Yourself Web Publishing With HTML in 14 Days, Laura LeMay, Sams, 1999

WEB SITES WITH HTML TUTORIALS

HTML: An Interactive Tutorial for Beginners
  www.davesite.com/webstation/html

Writing HTML
  www.mcli.dist.maricopa.edu/tut/

WebMonkey: Authoring HTML Basics
www.webmonkey.com/teachingtool/

HTML Primer
www.htmlprimer.com

FREE WEB SITES

AOL Hometown
http://hometown.aol.com

Geocities
www.geocities.yahoo.com

Homestead
www.homestead.com

Tripod
www.tripod.lycos.com/build/sitebuilder/

POWERTOOL 6—MAKE A PERSONAL MISSION STATEMENT

BOOKS ON BUSINESS PLANS

Anatomy of a Business Plan: A Step-by-Step Guide to Starting Smart, Building the Business and Securing Your Company's Future; Linda Pinson, Dearborn Trade, 2001

The One Page Business Plan: Start With a Vision, Build a Company; James T. Horan Jr., Jim Horan, Rebccca S. Shaw, ed., One Page Business Plan Co., 1998

The Successful Business Plan: Secrets and Strategies, Rhonda M. Abrams and Eugene Kleiner, Running R Media, 2000

Your First Business Plan: A Simple Question and Answer Format Designed to Help You Write Your Own Plan; Joseph Covello, Brian J. Hazelgren, Sourcebooks Trade, 1998

WEB SITES ON BUSINESS PLANS

Bplans.com
www.bplans.com

SBA: Starting Your Business: Business Plans
www.sba.gov/starting/indexbusplans.html

About.com Entrepreneurs
www.entrepreneurs.about.com/smallbusiness/entrepreneurs/cs/businessplans

POWERTOOL 7—BE A ROLE MODEL, BE A MENTOR

BOOKS ON MENTORING

Mentoring Heroes: 52 Fabulous Women's Paths to Success and the Mentors Who Empowered Them, Mary K. Doyle, 3E Press, 2000

The Mentor's Guide: Facilitating Effective Learning Relationships, Lois J. Zachary, Jossey-Bass, 2000

Woman to Woman: Preparing Yourself to Mentor, Edna Ellison and Tricia Scribner, 1999

WEB SITES ON MENTORING

Learning Mentors (articles/resources)
www.fastcompany.com/online/resources/learnment.html

Women's Ways of Mentoring (article)
www.fastcompany.com/online/17/womentoring.html

SBA Mentoring: Women's Network for Entrepreneurial Training Mentoring Program (WNET)
www.sbaonline.sba.gov/womeninbusiness/wnet.html

POWERTOOL 8—NURTURE YOUR NETWORK

BOOKS ABOUT NETWORKING

Breakthrough Networking: Building Relationships That Last, Lillian D. Bjorseth, Duoforce Enterprises, 1996

Fifty-Two Ways to Reconnect, Follow-Up and Stay in Touch When You Don't Have Time to Network, Anne Baber, Lynne Waymon, Waymon and Associates, 1993

Make Your Connections Count: The Six-Step System to Build Your Meganetwork, Melissa Giovagnoli, Dearborn, Trade, 1994

Power Networking: 55 Secrets for Personal and Professional Success, Donna Fisher, Sandy Vilas, Bard Press, 2000

The Secrets of Savvy Networking: How to Make the Best Connections for Business and Personal Success, Susan Roane, Warner Books, 1993

WEB SITES ABOUT NETWORKING

Five Keys to Networking Success (article)
www.businessknowhow.com/marketing/network1.htm

About.com Career Planning (resources)
www.careerplanning.about.com/careers/careerplanning/cs/networking/

Introduction to Networking (articles)
www.profnet.org/report.net

POWERTOOL 9—BE COMFORTABLE WITH POWER

BOOKS ON PUBLIC SPEAKING

In the Spotlight: Overcome Your Fear of Public Speaking and Performing, Janet E. Esposito, Strong Books 2000

101 Secrets of Highly Effective Speakers: Controlling Fear, Commanding Attention, Caryl Rae Krannich, 1998

101 Ways to Captivate a Business Audience, Sue Gaulke, AMACOM, 1996

7 Steps to Fearless Speaking, Lilyan Wilder, John Wiley & Sons, 1999

WEB SITES FOR PUBLIC SPEAKERS

Toastmasters
www.toastmasters.org

National Speakers Association
www.nsaspeaker.org

Public Speaking Resources
www.college.hmco.com/communications/public/index.htm

POWERTOOL 10—GIVE BACK

BOOKS ABOUT GIVING

Common Internet, Common Good: Creating Value Through Business and Social Sector Partnerships, Shirley Sagawa et. al., Harvard Business School Press, 1999

Don't Just Give It Away: How to Make the Most of Your Charitable Giving, Renata J. Rafferty and Paul Newman, Chandler House Press, 1999

Inspired Philanthropy, Tracy Gary et. al., Chardon Press, 1998

WEB SITES FOR ONLINE GIVING

GreaterGood.com
   www.greatergood.com

iGive.com
   www.igive.com

iReachOut.com
   www.ireachout.com/

Shop for Change
   www.shopforchange.com

VolunteerMatch.com
   www.volunteermatch.com

INDEX

A

Accomplishments
    acknowledging, 154-155, 159
    downplaying, 146–147, 153
    talking about, 137
Ad agencies, 25, 29
Adams, Mary, 59
Adobe PhotoShop, 83
Adventuring, solo, 50–55
Advice columnist, 48
Advocates for the Homeless, 168
Aesthetics of your environment, 38
Affirmations, "power tools" as, 3–4
Aho, Lorraine, 61–62
AKB & Associates, 151–153
Alexander, Rachel, 27
Aligning work and life, 30
Alize Public Relations, 109–110
All MarCom, LLC, 100–102
Allen, Heidi, 81
America Online, 103
American Marketing Association, 123
American Women's Economic
    Development (AWED), 132
Appendix, 184–193
Apricot, the (poem), 28
Army experiences, 48–49
Art of Self Direction, 95
Asset, business, 55
Athlete, professional, 27
Attitude, "I can do anything," 32
AudioBasket, 52
Autonomous Fem Coach, 48

Azzarto, Mary, 30

B

Bad situations, staying in, 31
Bananas, ditching, 29
Bank balance as motivator, 18
Bankruptcy, 59
Barr, Roseanne, 145
Battered women, teaching technologi-
    cal job skills to, 92
Beacon, your mission as, 97
Becker, Margaret, 163
Belief, 17
Belly dancing, 45
Berke, Alison, 153–155
Berman, Suzi, 64
Bernard Marketing Associates, 125–
    126
Bernard, Debbie, 125–126
Berners-Lee, Tim, 6
Beyond Ink, 16
Billboard, "be a walking," 142
Bindis, 23
BioSpace.Com, Inc., 7
Book recommendations, 101–102, 154,
    164–165
    business plans, 114
    creative writing and journaling, 76
    mentoring, 129
    networking, 143
    public speaking, 162
    travel and business, 57
    women's stories, 20

Boss
    as mentor, 125
    bad, 32
Boy's club, business networks as, 146
Bragging, 154–155
Branding oneself, 118, 159
Breathe, not forgetting to, 75
BridgeLight Group, 124–125
Brown, Alexandria K., 151–153
Bruce, Patsy, 70–72
Business Development Group, Inc., 134
Business plan
    personal philosophy as guide to, 110
    solidity of, 54
Business startup as symbolic gesture, 61
Businesswomen, issues unique to, 120, 123
Busy is better, 19
bworks.com, 153
By The Hour, Inc., 141

C

Caillet, Janice, 103–104
Cameron, Caryn, 46–47
Career
    failure, reinventing oneself out of, 72
    unhappiness, 95
Caregiver's Comfort book, 70
Caregiver's Comfort Creations, LLC, 69–70
Carey, Sandra, 39
Carmagnol, Caroline, 109–110
Catalyst, storytelling as, 8–10

CEO's, women, 118
Cerebral Palsy Research Foundation (CPRF), 163
Certification, 42
Challenging *vs.* fierce work environment, 109
Change
    -a-holic, 24
    agent, becoming your own, 30
    agents, mini, 35–36
    as opportunity, 25
    drastic, 8–10
    initiating, 25
    learning, 55
    openness to, 35
    purposeful, 23
Chaos, creating, 25
Checklist
    be comfortable with power, 161
    change, 38
    crisis, 76
    give back, 173
    learn constantly, 57
    make a personal mission statement, 114
    nurture your network, 143
    role model, mentor, 129
    share your stories, 20
    technology as your tool, 93
Checklists
    be a role model, be a mentor, 130
Clarity of mission, 108–109
Classes outside of your field, taking, 44
Clients, original ideas for, 41
Clinton, Hillary Rodham, 153
Cloudhawk Management Consultants,

LLC, 16
Cloudman, Catherine H., 16
Co-mentoring, 123
Coaching Circles, 103–104
Coaching, personal, corporate,
      executive, 104
Cobb, Liz, 53
College
      advanced degrees, 44
      community, 42, 89
      continuing education programs in,
            55
      degree, finishing, 32
      degree, value in earning, 42
Columbia Records, 82
Communications 21, Inc., 39
Communities, networking as building,
      138
Community Partners, 168
Competitive nature, 16, 19, 109
Computer Coach, Inc., 43
Consciousness as key to realization,
      100
Consultancy, 26
Consulting Software and Services
      (DCSS), 163–165
Contacts
      database of, 142
      sharing, 135 (See also Networking)
Cook Downing, Julie, 69–70
Corporate
      dream job, quitting, 106–107
      hierarchy, game of, 107
      secretary to executive, 123
      support, charitable, 169–170
      world, ditching, 124

Country Inn, 71
Covey, Stephen, 77
Creativity, 19
      cultivating, 44, 45
      honoring your, 8
      in conversation, 16–20, 36
      in writing and journaling, 76
Crisis
      as new beginning, 73
      overcoming, 59–77
Critical Insights, Inc., 16
Critical thinking, 19
Culture shock, Saudi Arabian, 53–54
Curiosity, childlike, 55
Curriculum vitae, 156–157
Cybergrrl, Inc., 24, 60, 97
      accidental mentors, 106
      mission statement, 106
      networking with name tags, 141
      using media coverage to inspire
            others, 121
      web site for women, 81
Cystic Fibrosis Foundation (CTF), 169

D

D Media, 64
Dale Carnegie courses, 43
Daughters, role model for, 145
Day job, leaving your, 29
DCSS Ability (DCSSA), 163
Death, company, 10
Defeat
      claiming, 25
      refusal to accept, 31
del Pico, Phyllis, 88, 90
Demoralization, 107

DesignWritePresentations, 41–42
Desires, list of, 109–110
Difficulties, learning from, 27
Digital "yenta," 46, 141
Disabilities
    advocacy company, 66–68
    employing people with, 167
    high-tech career training for people
        with, 163
Divorce, reinventing yourself after, 70–
    72
Donation-linked products, 166
Dream to mission, 96–115
Dress for Success, 172–173
Driscoll, Helen, 85–86
Duke, Heather, 23

E

e-commerce web site, 23
e-mail
    correspondence, 87
    introductions, 133
    mentoring, 120–121
E-Myth Academy, 42–43
Earle, Carey, 97–99
Earthlink, 86
eBay, 23, 118
EC12, 168–170
Education Companion (Internet newslet-
    ter), 84
EKindness.com, 84
Endurance lessons, 72
Epstein, Randy, 87–88, 90
Essential "You" day, 74–75
Ethics before money, 108
eTime Solutions, Inc., 32

ETravelplan.com, 165–166
European companies and American
    markets, 109
Events Unlimited, 71
Excel (spreadsheets), 82
Expectations, fulfilling others', 27
experience.com, 121–122

F

Failure
    as part of path, 4
    reinvention after marriage, 72
Faith as source of strength, 17, 72, 73
Family
    and divorce, 72
    coaching, 48
    encouragement, 71
    focus, 101
    needs of, 17
    role model for, 145
    single parent, 32
Fast Company magazine, 36
Fear
    facing, 61
    of technology, overcoming, 84
    revealing, 4
    unlearning, 32
Fem Coach, autonomous, 48
Feng shui, 36–38
    books on, 38
Field trips
    staff, 36
Film
    animation, 32, 119
    chronicling women in technical
        fields, 85

documentary, 8, 10
production, 34
Financial independence, 101
Fine Paper Company, 85–86
Fiorina, Carly, 118
Firestorm, Oakland Hills, 72–73
Fisher, Kim, 52
Fitzgerald, MaryEllen, 16
Fixers, women as, 31
Flex-time, 36
Flexibility
cultivating, 52
in work structure, 109
Internet technology as key to, 90
of entrepreneurship, 69
of online communication, 81
staff, 81
Floren, Jennifer, 121–122
Focus
ability to, 125
keeping your, 67, 100
Follow-up, 135
Fortune 500 convention events, 71
Forum for Women Entrepreneurs, 138
Forums, female only, 149–151
Free spirit, 62
Freelance writing, 72. *See also* Writing
Friends, importance of, 72
Frisky's Wildlife and Primate Sanctuary, 168–169
Fun, remembering to have, 68

G

Gain through loss, 63
Gardening as networking paradigm, 143

Gaucher's Disease, 65
Gen Xers, 9
Gender
difference in business, 146
issues, 149–151, 153
Genetic disorder, 65
Gerber, Michael, 43
Ging, Nancy, 49
Girl's network, cultivating, 146
Girlgeeks, 85
Giving
art of, 165–166
back, 163–174
principle of, 135
Global Business Association, 138
Goals
setting, 72
steps toward achieving, 100
Goldmacher, Sharon, 39
Good-girl manners as hindrance, 149
Graphic design, 41
into Web design, 79
program, Adobe PhotoShop, 83
Gratitude as motivator, 17
Greencrest Marketing, 26
Guide, women's need for, 124. *See also* Circles, Mentor, Networking

H

Hang-glider pilot, 27
Hanna, Kristine, 85
Hardball, negotiation, 46
Harmel, Christine, 45–46, 141
Harris, Cynthia, 72–73
Harrison, Jill, 104–105
Harsch-Porter, Sherry, 44

Harvest Consulting Group, 97–99

Heart's desire, shifts in, 101

Heaton, Lissa, 125

Helgesen, Sally, 131

Help, asking for without fear or guilt, 137

Hewlett-Packard, 118

Hierarchy. See Corporate

Holistic
  learning style, 44
  mentoring, 124

Holzschlag, Molly, 47

Home, working at, 88, 90

Homeless women, education and job training for, 168

Honoring yourself, 175–177

Hope, women's, 73

HTML
  classes, 47, 60
  language, 84
  self-taught, 90
  tutorial Web sites, 93

I

IBM, 120

iCan.com, 66–68

Ideas
  underutilization of, 31
  value of corny, 74

Illness, overcoming, 64–65

Imaginestation, 89

Incentive compensation programs, 19

Incentive Systems, 53

Incorporating, 26, 84

Indian body adornment (bindis), 23

Inner
  direction, 17
  peace, 8–9

Inside circle, 134

Intention, examining one's own, 11

Interactive Resource, The, 45–46

International Speakers Bureau (ISB), 68–69

Internet
  as tool for non-technical business, 87
  early years of, 80–81
  familiarity with lingo of, 91
  skills, sharing, 91–92
  start-up, 32 (*See also* Online, Web)

Internet Presence Consulting, Inc., 117

Investor relations executive, 123

Invitesite.com, 86

Isolation, ending businesswomen's, 15–16

Isole Development, 104–105

IT workers, demand for qualified, 85

Itec Resources, 100

J

Jagemann, Paula, 168–170

Jagged Edge Mountain Gear, 89–90

James, Jennifer, 23

Job loss, recovery from, 62

Journal
  for healing, 75–76
  keeping in a crisis, 62–63

Joy, finding, 176

JRY Development Corp., 83

K

Kahn, Brenda, 82–83

Kat and Mouse Web Design, 79
Kay, Andrea, 95
Kennedy, Anne, 16, 19
King, Jennifer C., 7
Knowledge Hound, LLC, 81–82
Knowledge vs. wisdom, 39
KPMG, 29
Kruss, Lisa, 117

L

La Femme (Female Executives Making
	It in Maine), 20
Ladylike behavior, 147, 153
Lally, Pauline, 42
Lane, Jenai, 8–10
Lawlor, Michelle, 84
Leadership development program,
	business, 39
Leads, sharing, 133
Learning, 39–58
	love of, 19
	never too late for, 88
	nontraditional, 40, 43–45
	on the job, 46–47
	project management, 42
	returning to school, 41–42
	turbo, 40
	value of traditional, 41
LeMay, Laura, 47
Lemmons, Michelle, 68–69
Lewis, Beth, 43–44
Life
	altering change, 27
	on own terms, 145
	story titles, 13–14
Linguistics degree, 49

Listening, 125
	as key to learning, 43
Lithuania, doing business in, 52–53
Long range planning, implementing,
	42
Long, Kathy, 79
Love-Track.com, 104
Low-income women into workforce,
	172–173
Loyalty, 26
Lublin, Nancy, 173
Luchansky Communications, 123–124
Lutchanksy, Robin, 123–124

M

Macromedia, 119
Mad Gab's, 167–168
Madame Curie, 117
Madonna, 118
Maine Women and Girls Foundation,
	168
Male dominated fields, women in, 43
Male/female dynamic, 149–151, 153
*Mamas Don't Let Your Babies Grow Up to
	Be Cowboys*, 71
Mantra, motto as, 112. *See also* Mission,
	Motto
Maori song of support, 12
Marketing communications firm, 102–
	103
Marketing Works, Inc., 25
Martha Stewart, 118
Martin, Elaine, 156
Mary Kay Ash, 175
Matchmaking, 142. *See also* Network-
	ing

Matthews, Carment, 48–49

McCall Media and Marketing, Inc., 155

McCall, Kimberly L., 155

McGoodwin, Wendy L., 157

McIvor, Gwen, 124–125

Mechanical engineering degree, 42

Media kit, creating your own, 157–159

Meecham, Sally, 131

Meetings, exploration and discovery, 36

Melchionda, Gabrielle, 167–168

Mentoring
    as opening doors, 126
    e-mail, 120–121
    national organizations for, 123
    programs, 122
    searching for female, 120
    tips, 122–123
    women into IT field, 85

Merrill, Christina, 16, 19–20

Mirrer, Candy, 138

MirrerSearch.com, 138

Mission, 95–115

Mission statement
    combining personal and profes-
        sional, 98, 102, 106
    formalizing, 103

Mock "non-disclosure agreements," 15

Modeling, 33

Moon, Kate, 11, 16

Morrison, Toni, 156

Mother/daughter coach, 48

Motivation, discussion of, 16–19

Motivational speakers, list of female, 77

Motivational speaking, 7

Motivators, deadlines and debt, 18, 19

Motto
    as summary of your mission, 104–
        106
    displaying, 112

Multimedia branding, 118

Musson, Sandy, 141

My Red Shoes, LLC, 87–88

N

Nashville Scenic, 71

Navy-brat, 24

Necessity, sheer, 25

Need/give philosophy, 136–137, 138

Needs, sacrificing, 34

Negotiation hardball, 46

Networking, 131–144
    circles, creating, 139–141
    events, organizing, 15–21
    name tags, 141–142
    sharing information while, 135
    solutions company, 84

New Zealand, 11–13

Newsletter
    Internet-based, 84
    publisher, 48
    quarterly, 31

Newspaper column, weekly, 95

Nonprofit donations, 166

Non-techie to techie, 82

O

O'Brien, Chris, 41

O'Neil, Heather, 165–166

Obstacles, internally imposed, 1–2, 4

Online
    bill-paying, 87

community, 85
company research, 87–88
courses, 43, 55, 58
interactive Web site, 85
knowledge, teaching, 92
music distribution, 83
OPEN class worlds, 28
Opening doors for protégé, 126
Original, be an, 145
Orit, 102–103
Outsourcing, 26

P

PAB Corporation, 70–72
Partners in Life, Inc., 103–104
Partnership
 ceremonies, 104
 dissolution of, 26
Party Personnel, LLC, 59
Pasquall, Lorraine M., 89
Passion in life and work, 102
Patterson, Patricia (Trish), 163–165
PayMYBills.com, 87
Payroll, making, 18
Personal
 challenges, adapting profession to
  address, 70
 coaches, 42
 development seminars, 44
 growth, relationships as barrier to,
  70
Personal project
 be a mentor, 128–130
 business plan for life, 112–113
 choose a cause, 170–172
 find a mentor, 126–128

make your own media kit, 157–159
motto making, 110–111
name tag tricks, 141–142
play matchmaker, matchmaker, 142
speak in public, 159–161
spring clean for charity, 172–173
write your curriculum vitae, 156–
 157
Phoenix rising metaphor, 72–73
Physically handicapped high-tech
 career training, 163
Pipefitter license, 42
Piping Systems, 42
PMS, 17
Polo, professional, 29
Porter Bay Group, 44
Positive
 attitude, 100
 change, 27
 opportunity, out of negative
  situations, 72
Potential, helping others discover their,
 95
Power
 lunch, 16–20
 wielding your, 145–162
Powertools
 definition of, 1–7
 summary of, 177
PowerTools as "How-to" manual, 5–6
Praxis Consulting, 46–47
Priorities, reexamining, 59
Product innovation, 8, 9
Professional
 crisis, turning around, 61–63
 setback, healing from, 7

Professional Business Women of
  California, 8
Profoundia, 23
Public relations coordinator, 25
Public Relations, LH3, Inc., 105
Public speaking, 36, 48
  national association of, 161
  practicing, 159–161
Purpose, living your, 104

Q

Queen of networking, 133. *See also*
  Networking
Quenemoen, Paula, 89–90
Quicken.com, 87

R

Radle, Joy, 100–102
Rainmakers, 134
Rajan, Geetha P., 100
Rebuilding, 62
RecruitersOnCall.com, 88
Relationship coaches, 104
Relationships
  business, 100
  cultivating long-term, 134
  emotional support, importance of,
    124, 125
  overemphasis upon for women, 70–
    72
Remedios, Tamara, 45
Research, 19
  e-commerce companies, 63
Resilience, 72
Respect, Inc., 8
Restaurant reviewing, 72

Returning to work, 79
Robbins, Anthony, 48, 77
Role models, finding, 118
Rolodex, "living, breathing, walking,"
  132
Rosen, Lucy, 132, 134, 140
Rude awakenings, 70
Rule breaking, 145

S

SacredHome.com, 61
SBA (Small Business Administration),
  63, 89
SBDC (Small Business Development
  Center), 89
Schanzer, Mary, 59
Scher, Laura, 166–167
SCORE volunteers, 63
Search engine, human, 86
Self
  care, 18
  discipline, 17
  discovery, 48
  forgetting, as survival mechanism,
    74–75
  giving to, 165–166
  image, 70
  limiting beliefs, overcoming, 50
  promotion, at ease with, 139
  respect, 50
  sabotage, 152
Serene Samurai, 48
Set building, 71
Shelley, Mary, 95
Show and Tell, grown-up version of, 36
Silicon Valley, 73

Slinger, the, 66

Slowing down, 63

Smart Catalog, 16

Smelling the roses, 39, 111

Social enterprise programs, 163

Social responsibility, incorporating into work/business, 167–170

Socially responsible spending, 166–167

Sole proprietorship, 26

Solitude, 50–51

Solo adventures, planning and taking, 56–57

Songwriting team, husband and wife, 71–72

Sowaal, Alice, 257

Special events company, 71

Spence Publishing, 145

Spence, Stephanie, 145

Staff, creating flexibility for self and, 36

Stier, Brenda K, 25

Stock options, 32

Storytelling
power of, 7–21
sunday brunch, 15–16

Strategic planning, 42

Strategy Associates, 73

Strength, position of, 152

Success
external trappings of, 63
motto for, 104–105
overcoming obstacles to, 1–2, 4
personal definitions of, 4
women's stumbling blocks to, 124

Support
active, 133

surrounding self with, 155

Suppression of talent, 31

Surviving and thriving, 65

T

Taker *vs.* giver, 134–135

Tanaka, Patrice, 120

Technical school, 43–44

Technology
as tool, 81
definition of, 86
tackling, 79–94
women overcoming fear of, 84

Telecommuting, 36

Television production company, 71

Toastmasters, 161

Tompkins Benefit Group, 106–108

Tompkins, Debbie, 106–109

Tooting your own horn, 155, 157

Total New York, 103

Trade school, 42

Tradeshow press kits, 73

Transformation through crisis, 72, 73

Traveldonkey Limited, 131

Traveling alone, 51

True
goals, 97
self, honoring, 175–177

Turbo
change lifestyle, 24
learning mode, 40

Turtle Island Web Design, 49

Type A personality learns to reflect, 53

U

Urgency addiction, 19

V

Vacation
   scheduling, 166
   taking, 39
Valentine, Anne, 16
Values
   honoring though your business, 27
   identifying core, 108
   not compromising personal, 167
   sharing, 109
Van Arnem, Heidi, 66–68
Venture capital, skills in obtaining, 54
ViA, Inc., 16
Video editing, 85
Vision statement, 97–98, 104. *See also*
   Mission statement
Vision, own *vs.* company, 9–10
Visualization and goal setting, 72
Voice, women finding their, 149–151
VolunteerMatch.com, 171

W

Walkabout Comfort Shoe Store, 11, 16
Web building. *See* Web design, Web
   development, Web Site
Web design
   business, part-time, 46
   courses in, 41
   software company, 120
Web development, 82
   teaching self basics of, 90–91, 93
Web site
   building project, 90–91
   free, 93
   recommendations
      "Herstory," 20–21

business plans
   mentoring, 130
   networking, 143
   online giving, 173
Webgrrls International, global
   networking group, 136–137
Webgrrls, Inc., forum for women, 151
WebMonkey.com, 47
Weeding and seeding your network,
   141, 144
Weldon, Katherine, 32
Welfare-to-work program, mentoring
   women at, 92
Whitman, Meg, 118
Williams, Terry Tempest, 7
Williamson, Marianne, 152
WiReD Magazine, 119
Wisdom, sharing of, 12
WOMANROCK.com, 82
Women
   and power, 151–153
   and technological skills, 79–94
   and the constraint of being
      ladylike, 147, 153
   as fixers, 31
   entrepreneurs, 8
   honoring themselves, 175–177
   in business, isolation of, 15–16
   in workplace, uniqueness of, 123
   on the Fast Track networking
      group, 132–133
   specific issues, speakers addressing,
      77
Women business enterprise certification, 42
Women in Development, 138

Women in Technology, Inc., 138
Women's
character, 73
hope, 73
lives, Internet as powerful tool for, 106
multiple roles, 117
need to be heard, 149
perseverence, 73
solo travels, books about, 57
stories, book recommendations, 20
wisdom, 12
Women's business organization membership, 122–123, 131
Women's Leaders Network, 12
Word (word processing), 82
Work
enjoying, 17–18
environment, 36–38
Working Assets, 166–167
World Economic Forum, 138
Writing
all kinds of, 72
as healing, 75–76
it down, 98, 100
queries, 97
skills, courses in, 41
your life story, book recommendations, 20

X

Xplore Communications, 45

Y

Young, Janet R., 83–84

Z

Zeal Co., 9
Zemaitis, Kathleen, 139
Ziglar, Zig, 77
Zimmerman, Bonnie, 157
Zine Communications, 139
Zine, WOMANROCK.com, 82
Zukav, Gary, 11

LIVING THE *POWERTOOLS*—INTERACTIVELY

The best way to put something you read in a book into action is to have ways to interact with other people who have read the same book and believe in the message.

Here are some ways you can bring the *PowerTools* to life.

SUBSCRIBE TO THE POWERTOOLS *E-MAIL LISTS*

These are two lists you can subscribe to for free that will keep the *PowerTools* alive for you long after you've read the book.

1. The *PowerTools* News List

Get a monthly dose of tips, inspiring stories, and up-dates on Aliza Sherman's appearances and workshops. And if you have something you'd like to submit to this announcement list for possible publication, e-mail news@mediaegg.com.

2. The *PowerTools* Talk List

Being able to talk with other women in business about issues you are facing each day is a valuable way of not only getting support and inspiration, but helping others in the process. Do it with the convenience of e-mail!

Join this discussion list moderated by Aliza Sherman and Alison Berke Morano to expand your network.

Instructions on subscribing to these lists can be found online at:

www.womenspowertools.com/lists.html

SHARE YOUR POWERTOOLS STORIES

Have an inspiring story that you'd like to see published on the WOMENSPOWERTOOLS.COM web site and share with women around the world?

Submit a brief summary of your story to stories@mediaegg.com for consideration.

Stories can include your photograph and a link to your business web site.

START A POWERTOOLS GROUP

Sometimes, there is nothing like sitting with other women—in person—to talk about the *PowerTools* and the issues you face in business and life. Start a regular gathering of women in your area, using the principles of the *PowerTools* as your discussion guide.

For more information about starting a *PowerTools* Group, go to: www.womenspowertools.com/groups.html

Let us know when you start one and where you are located so we tell you when Aliza Sherman is appearing in your city. Special private gatherings can be arranged with the author, logistics permitting.

Stay Motivated. Get Inspired.
Go to
WWW.WOMENSPOWERTOOLS.COM.